Home/ELT/Sample Pa
Teacher's Resou

- Audio Script
- SB Answer Key
- Additional Exercises (& Answ. Key).

Have
YourSay!

Have Your Say!

Second Edition

Communication Activities

Irene S. McKay

OXFORD
UNIVERSITY PRESS

OXFORD

UNIVERSITY PRESS

8 Sampson Mews, Suite 204, Don Mills, Ontario M3C 0H5
www.oupcanada.com

Oxford University Press is a department of the University of Oxford. It furthers the University's
objective of excellence in research, scholarship,and education by publishing worldwide in

Oxford   New York

Auckland Cape Town Dar es Salaam Hong Kong Karachi Kuala Lumpur Madrid
Melbourne Mexico City Nairobi New Delhi Shanghai Taipei Toronto

With offices in

Argentina Austria Brazil Chile Czech Republic France Greece Guatemala Hungary Italy Japan
Poland Portugal Singapore South Korea Switzerland Thailand Turkey Ukraine Vietnam

Oxford is a trade mark of Oxford University Press in the UK and in certain other countries

Published in Canada by Oxford University Press

Library and Archives Canada Cataloguing in Publication

McKay, Irene
Have your say! : intermediate communication activities / Irene S. McKay. –2nd ed.

ISBN 978-0-19-543261-9

1. English language—Textbooks for second language learners. 2. English language—Spoken English—
Problems, exercises, etc.—Juvenile literature. 3. Communication—Problems, exercises, etc. I. Title.

PE1128.M198 2010   428.3'4   C2009-907126-6

Cover image: ildogesto/iStock Photography

Audio Credits
Thank you to the Canadian Broadcasting Corporation for permission to use the audio clips in Chapters 7 and 8.

Photo Credits
1 iStockphoto.com / Dmitriy Shironosov; 7 iStockphoto.com / Winston Davidian; 17 iStockphoto.com / Suprijono Suharjoto;
24 (left) iStockphoto.com / Vernon Wiley, (right) Andy Kainz Photography; 26 (left) Ryan Kelly, (right) Popperfoto; 30 Lebrecht
Music and Arts Photo Library / Alamy; 35 (left) iStockphoto.com / Kevin Tavares, (centre) iStockphoto.com / Kirill Bodrov, (right)
iStockphoto.com / Lya Cattel; 42 iStockphoto.com / Sevgi Ulutas; 49 iStockphoto.com / Nikolay Mamluke; 58 iStockphoto.com /
Alija; 61 iStockphoto.com / Zhang Bo; 66 iStockphoto.com / Wouter van Caspel; 67 iStockphoto.com / Daniel Rodriguez;
69 iStockphoto.com / Mikhail Kokhanchikov; 70 iStockphoto.com / Mark Rose; 72 iStockphoto.com / Jim Jurica; 80 (left)
iStockphoto.com / grimgram, (right) iStockphoto.com / Mario Jesús Alvariño; 85 iStockphoto.com / Marilyn Nieves; 87 iStockphoto.
com / Mark Stay; 101 iStockphoto.com / Stephen Dumayne; 107 iStockphoto.com / Andreja Donko; 112 iStockphoto.com / Dan
Eckert; 114 Colin Anderson; 127, 131–2 iStockphoto.com / Yuri Schipakin; 143 (left) iStockphoto.com / Hannu Liivaar, (right)
iStockphoto.com / Cristian Lazzari; 159 iStockphoto.com / Tomas Bercic; 162 iStockphoto.com / Chris Schmidt; 169 iStockphoto.
com / Elena Korenbaum; 176 iStockphoto.com / Athos Boncompagni; 187 iStockphoto.com / Andrea Hill; 194 iStockphoto.com /
Zhang Bo; 199 (left) iStockphoto.com / Slobo Mitic, (right) iStockphoto.com / Wesley Pohl; 211 iStockphoto.com / Benjamin Goode

Oxford University Press is committed to our environment. This book is printed on Forest Stewardship Council certified paper,
harvested from a responsibly managed forest.

Printed and bound in Canada.

1 2 3 4 — 14 13 12 11

Dedication

For my mother and father, whose efforts and determination have always inspired me.

Acknowledgements

I want to thank the many ESL/EFL students I have taught, both at George Brown College and in other institutions. I am also indebted to the many teachers I have trained at George Brown College and in other contexts. The amazing classroom experiences that I have had enabled me to produce this book. Working with dedicated and motivated learners has inspired me to produce materials which I believe address ESL learner needs and interests.

I also want to express my gratitude to all my friends and colleagues in ESL and EFL for continuing to make this field such a stimulating and exciting one. I am grateful to George Brown College of Arts and Technology for providing a fertile and motivating environment for my work.

Table of Contents

	Listening	Language Functions	Speaking and Pronunciation	Grammar Structures
Chapter 1: **Tell Us a Little about Yourself: Giving Information and Descriptions** **Page 1**	1. Conversation: Two students 2. Radio interview: Good/poor language learners	1. Introductions: Yourself/others 2. Giving personal information 3. Describing personal characteristics 4. Handling problems in communication: Asking for repetition or clarification 5. Complimenting 6. Inviting 7. Conversation openers	Word stress in words with common suffixes	1. Simple present: Facts, habits 2. Present progressive 3. Adjectives, colours 4. *would like*
Chapter 2: **Experiences and Achievements** **Page 24**	1. Conversation: Famous women 2. Radio travel report	1. Narrating/talking about past events 2. Encouraging conversation 3. Paraphrasing 4. Discussing similarities and differences 5. Explaining	Pronunciation of regular past tense endings	1. Simple past 2. *used to/would*: Past habits 3. Comparative and superlative forms of adjectives 4. Transition words for stating reasons and for explaining results
Chapter 3: **Friends, Families, and Relationships** **Page 49**	1. Lecture: Friendship 2. Talk show interview: Families, census information	1. Requesting and responding to requests 2. Gaining time to think 3. Describing a process 4. Expressing necessity	Basic intonation patterns	1. Modals: *can, will, could, would* 2. Indirect questions 3. *must/have to/had to*
Chapter 4: **Food and Lifestyles** **Page 78**	1. Radio talk show: Likes and dislikes in food 2. Quiz show: Idioms in food 3. Lecture: Attaining health and happiness	1. Talking about events in the indefinite past 2. Expressing likes and dislikes 3. Expressing opinions, agreeing, disagreeing, supporting opinions	Stressed and unstressed words (content/function words)	1. Present perfect: Indefinite past 2. Verbs taking gerunds/infinitives

	Listening	Language Functions	Speaking and Pronunciation	Grammar Structures
Chapter 5: **Leisure,** **Sports, and** **Entertainment** **Page 103**	1. Sports call-in show 2. Psychology lecture: Violence	1. Stating and asking about preferences 2. Expressing ability/inability 3. Expressing advisability/inadvisability 4. Expressing inadvisability, reprimanding 5. Expressing possibility, speculating	Linking words in connected speech	1. *would rather* 2. Modals: *can, could, was, were able to, should/shouldn't* 3. Modals of possibility: *might, could, may*
Chapter 6: **The Personal and** **the Professional,** **Emotions and** **Work** **Page 125**	1. Radio interview: Psychologist on emotions 2. Radio show: Panel discussion on dream jobs	1. Expressing probability and assumptions 2. Expressing emotions 3. Making and responding to suggestions 4. Giving complex descriptions 5. Adding Information and ideas 6. Interrupting 7. Restating Information 8. Describing skills, knowledge and abilities	More on linking words in connected speech	1. Modals of probability 2. Relative clauses 3. Question words + infinitives
Chapter 7: **Society and** **Culture** **Page 156**	1. CBC Radio interview: Roger Axtell on Gestures 2. CBC Radio show: Who Owns Ideas?	1. Making recommendations, predicting consequences 2. Apologizing, responding 3. Making complaints 4. Expressing warnings and prohibitions 5. Comparing and contrasting	Focus words and intonation	1. Conditionals 2. Subjunctive after *recommend, demand*, etc. 3. *mustn't; had better* 4. Conjunctions and conjunctive adverbs of contrast
Chapter 8: **Nature and the** **Environment** **Page 184**	1. CBC Radio interview: Elephants in Zoos 2. CBC radio show: Climate Refugees	1. Taking turns in conversation 2. Asking for and giving impersonal information 3. Expressing disapproval 4. Criticizing 5. Eliciting and analyzing opinions expressing degrees of certainty 6. Countering arguments, persuading 7. Expressing regret 8. Reporting information 9. Hypothesizing	Complex intonation patterns	1. Passive voice 2. Past of *should* 3. *be supposed to* 4. *wish*: Present/past/future 5. Reported speech 6. Conditionals

Introduction

To the Teacher

Have Your Say! is a course in listening and speaking for intermediate to advanced students. The 2nd Edition includes the popular features of the 1st Edition and adds much more, including pronunciation activities in each chapter.

Have Your Say! is based on the principles that learner-centredness and exposure to authentic, meaningful language in collaborative activities provide the means and motivation for learners to develop proficiency in oral communication. The materials have been designed to take learners from Benchmark 5 (Initial Intermediate Proficiency in Speaking and Listening) to Benchmark 9 (Initial Advanced Proficiency in Speaking and Listening) of the Canadian Language Benchmarks.

Features of the Text

Listening

Each chapter includes two or three listening activities related to the chapter's theme. Pre-listening tasks prepare students for what they will hear on the audio CD. Listening tasks require learners to focus on main ideas and on details. They also serve to introduce naturally occurring vocabulary items and idioms. Listening sections in Chapters 7 and 8 feature authentic material from Canadian Broadcasting Corporation (CBC) radio programs. This material prepares students for communication in real-life situations and presents a variety of engaging topics.

Speaking

After completing each listening activity, students engage in a variety of speaking tasks. These may be interviews in which there is an information or opinion gap; group activities in which students collaborate to achieve a goal; communication games; or role-plays. These activities are designed to encourage students to produce a great quantity of language. Questionnaires and short reading selections are also used to maintain interest and expose learners to authentic language.

Speaking activities are related to Communication Focus sections. The purpose of these sections is to introduce or review the language functions, gambits, or language structures that learners will need to use in the speaking activities. The aim is to encourage learners to produce certain language functions and structures at the same time that they are working on improving fluency.

Pronunciation

New in the 2nd Edition, each chapter includes extensive pronunciation activities. Numerous activities and examples appear on the audio CD. Students also practise pronunciation skills with each other in a variety of situations by sharing information and playing games.

Speaking and Listening Strategies

These short, informative sidebars focus student attention on strategies to use in listening and speaking. Teachers can use these as jumping-off points for discussion, and to raise the learners' awareness of their strategy use.

Self Evaluation

It is recognized that when learners take responsibility for their learning, their use of effective language learning strategies and their proficiency increases. Each chapter in *Have Your Say!* ends with a self evaluation section which allows students to reflect on what they have learned and on what they still need to improve. These sections can be completed individually or they can be used as a basis for discussion or journal writing.

Other Components

 ## Audio CDs

The *Have Your Say! Audio CDs* contain three discs packed with listening material, including authentic recordings from CBC radio programs. The CDs also contain a variety of pronunciation activities to model and reinforce the patterns and intonations of North American English.

 ## Companion Website

The *Have Your Say! Companion Website* includes a complete Answer Key as well as activities that give students additional practice with the language structures introduced throughout the book.

Practical and Theoretical Considerations

Some students and teachers worry that learners who speak to other learners will not improve their communication competency, but rather will learn each other's mistakes. For some time, research has indicated that this is not the case. Learners, whether speaking to native speakers or to non-native speakers, get the same quantity and quality of practice in the number of times that they speak and in the kinds of language functions and speech acts they engage in. It appears, then, that if teachers can involve students in producing as large a quantity of meaningful focused speech as possible, the students' abilities to understand and to communicate will improve.

Have Your Say! is based on the concept that learners need to be active and that they need to use the language to accomplish tasks. The text recognizes that learners need to take responsibility for their learning and that they need to stretch their competence in order to produce language which is appropriate and accurate. The activities involve learners in collaborating to produce meaningful language in an environment conducive to language acquisition. *Have Your Say!* also introduces learners to aspects of North American culture and conversation. It focuses attention on the learner and provides natural opportunities for interaction and communication.

Thinking and Talking

Work with a partner. Describe the people in the picture. What are they doing? What do you think they are saying? How do you think they feel?

Tell your partner about the first time you came to this school. What did you think of it? How did you feel? How have your ideas changed since then?

Read the following poem. How does the poet feel about introductions? Why do you think she feels this way? How do you feel about introductions?

I'm Nobody! Who are you?
by Emily Dickinson

I'm Nobody! Who are you?
Are you — Nobody — Too?
Then there's a pair of us!
Don't tell! they'd advertise — you know!

How dreary — to be — Somebody!
How public — like a Frog —
To tell one's name — the livelong June —
To an admiring Bog!

LISTENING STRATEGY

If you think about what you are going to hear, and try to predict what people will say, this may help your comprehension.

Listening 1

Before You Listen

1. Think about the last time you met someone new. Tell your partner where this took place. Who did you meet, and what did you learn about the person?

2. You will hear a conversation on the audio CD between two people who are meeting for the first time. Predict three pieces of information they will give about themselves.

   a) _____

   b) _____

   c) _____

Listening for the Main Ideas

Listen to the conversation on the audio CD once and answer these questions.

1. Where are the speakers?

2. What are two topics they talk about?

3. Which of your predictions was correct?

Listening Comprehension

Listen to the conversation again. Complete the following chart.

Man's name	_____
Woman's name	_____
What does she say about the students at the college?	_____
How does she get to the school?	_____
What are two things she does in the mornings?	_____
What does she offer to do?	_____
What information about the apartment building does she give him?	_____
What does she invite him to?	_____
What other things do they talk about?	_____

Personalizing

1. Tell your partner about the last time you moved to a new place. How did you find out about the transportation and about the area?

2. Think about the conversation you have just heard. In other countries, how do people introduce themselves and speak to each other when they meet for the first time? What body language do they use? What are some similarities and differences?

Vocabulary and Language Chunks

Write the number of the expression next to the meaning. After checking your answers, choose six expressions and write your own sentences.

Expressions

1. make friends
2. by the way
3. take a lot of time
4. in no time
5. all set
6. stay up
7. get up
8. get on
9. get to
10. in time
11. give someone a call
12. wait for
13. be into
14. look forward to
15. no big deal
16. drop by
17. have people over
18. tons of

Meanings

- [ ] arrive
- [ ] very quickly
- [ ] not go to bed
- [ ] board
- [ ] telephone someone
- [ ] await, expect
- [ ] become friends
- [ ] ready
- [ ] incidentally
- [ ] just before a set time or deadline
- [ ] like very much
- [ ] wake up and get out of bed
- [ ] require a long time
- [ ] a great deal of, lots of
- [ ] invite people to your house
- [ ] go to someone's place
- [ ] nothing very important
- [ ] anticipate, think pleasurably about something which will happen

Communication Focus: Introducing Yourself

Structures/Expressions	Examples	Responses
Hello, my name is . . .	Hello, I'm Cassie.	Hello, Cassie.
Hi, I'm . . .	Hi, I'm Cassie.	Hi.
Hi, I'd like to introduce myself . . .	Hi, I'd like to introduce myself. My name is Ryan Thomas.	(It's) nice to meet you.
Hi, I don't think we've met . . .	Hi, I don't think we've met. I'm Ryan Thomas.	(I'm) glad to meet you.
Let me introduce myself . . .	Let me introduce myself. I'm Ryan Thomas.	My name is Sarah. I'm Sarah.

More Formal

Hello, I don't believe we've met . . .	I don't believe we've met. I'm Helen Tang.	How do you do?
Allow me to introduce myself . . .	Allow me to introduce myself. My name is Bruce Ross.	Pleased to meet you.

Speaking Activity 1

Work in pairs. Number the sentences in the following conversations in the correct order and then practise saying them. Choose one of the conversations as a model and make up a conversation to introduce yourselves. Role-play your conversation for the class.

Conversation A

☐ Hi, I'm Sheila. I'm glad to meet you.

☐ That would be great! Let's do that. We can have coffee or a drink and practise our English. I'm really glad we met.

☐ I think it's difficult but it's lots of fun. I'm having a ball doing the activities.

☐ It's nice meeting you, too. How are you finding the work in the English course?

☐ Maybe we can get together after class one of these days, compare notes and share our ideas.

☐ It's keeping me busy. I enjoy it, but it's challenging. What about you?

☐ Hello, my name is Jackie. I'm in the same English class as you. I sit several rows behind you.

Conversation B

☐ Thanks for listening and for the advice.

☐ That's an excellent idea. I guess I need to make a complaint. Maybe there is a way to fix the problem.

☐ Pleased to meet you, Michael. I'm Diane Lawrence.

☐ Well, no, not really. I can't say that I do. What about you? Does the noise bother you, Michael?

☐ That's too bad. I'm sure there's a solution to it. Why don't you speak to the superintendent.

☐ Hello. Allow me to introduce myself. My name is Michael Rogers. I believe we live in the same building. I see you there all the time.

☐ Good luck!

☐ How do you do? I hope you don't mind if I ask you a question. Do you hear a lot of noise late at night in your apartment?

☐ Yes. It's a big problem for me. I hear the elevator and noises from the lobby. Sometimes the noise is so bad that I can't sleep.

Speaking Activity 2

Introduce yourself to the class. Tell them three things about yourself, two of which are not true. The person who guesses which statement is true takes the next turn.

Speaking Activity 3

As a class, stand in two circles, one circle inside the other. If you are in the outside circle, move clockwise. If you are in the inside circle, move counter-clockwise. The teacher will play some music. When the music stops or when the teacher claps his or her hands, stop moving.

Face your classmates in the other circle, shake hands, introduce yourselves, and talk. After several minutes the music will start again. When the music starts, move around in your circles. The music will start and stop several times. At the end of 15–20 minutes, report about one or two of the people you met.

Speaking Activity 4

Work in groups of three. Discuss the expressions in the following list and put them into the correct categories. Some of these are expressions we use when we meet people. Others are expressions we use to say good-bye. There are also expressions we use when we want to get a person's attention. You can also discuss and record other expressions that you have heard but which are not on the list. Put + next to expressions that you think are more formal and – next to those that you think are informal.

Hey!	What's up?	Have a good one.	Good afternoon.
Pardon me.	See you later.	Good evening.	Take care.
Hi there!	Good night.	Excuse me, can I ask a question?	How are things?
Good day.	So long.		Long time no see!
Bye now.	Have a good day.	I'm sorry to bother you.	Keep in touch!
How's it going?	Talk to you soon.		Good morning.

Greetings	**Saying Good-bye**	**Getting Attention**
_____	_____	_____
_____	_____	_____
_____	_____	_____
_____	_____	_____
_____	_____	_____
_____	_____	_____
_____	_____	_____

Grammar Note: Simple Present Tense for Facts and Habits

We can use the simple present tense to talk about facts, habits, and routines.

When we talk about habitual activities, we often use adverbs or phrases such as every day, every month, on Fridays, on Mondays, once in a while.

We can also use adverbs of frequency such as always, never, often, sometimes, usually, frequently, rarely.

Examples
Fact: Sam, have you met Cecile? She comes from Uruguay.
Habit or routine: This is Melinda. She usually goes jogging before she comes to school.

 Please go to the website for more practice with this structure.

Communication Focus: Introducing Others

Structures/Expressions	Examples
I would like to introduce . . .	George, I'd like to introduce Mathew. Mathew teaches photography.
I'd like you to meet . . .	Marta, I'd like you to meet Nicole. She speaks French.
Do you know . . . Have you met . . .	Doug, have you met Ruby? She works in the registration office.
This is . . .	Laura, this is Edward. He has an interesting hobby.

Speaking Activity 5

Work in pairs to conduct interviews with each other. Form the questions and then find out the answers. Then join another pair of students and introduce each other. Give some important information about the person you are introducing.

Information	Questions	Answers: Me	Answers: My Partner
Name? Nickname?	What is your name? Do you have a nickname?	_____	_____
Nationality/country/ city of birth?	_____	_____	_____
Languages spoken?	_____	_____	_____
Length of time in this city?	_____	_____	_____
Family status? Single/ married?	_____	_____	_____
Length of time studying English?	_____	_____	_____
Reasons for taking this course?	_____	_____	_____
Previous travel/ countries visited?	_____	_____	_____
Future plans/long term goals/ambitions?	_____	_____	_____
Problems in learning English?	_____	_____	_____
Interests/hobbies/sports?	_____	_____	_____
Past education/number of years/major/degrees?	_____	_____	_____
Other question(s)?	_____	_____	_____

Speaking Activity 6

Work in groups of four. List all the things you have in common (the ways in which you are similar). List all your differences. Think about habits, likes, dislikes, interests, family, past experiences, and opinions. You can also think about favourites—foods, places, activities, actors, movies, music, etc. The group which finds the most similarities and differences wins!

Speaking Activity 7

Work with a partner. Each of you will imagine a person you would like to be. This person is going to make a speech or presentation at a conference or business meeting. Interview your partner and fill in the chart.

Introduce your partner to the class. Make sure you include lots of interesting details in your introduction.

	Me	My Partner
Name		
Profession		
Nationality		
Accomplishment		
Hobbies/interests		
Topic of presentation/ speech		

Communication Focus: Conversation Openers—Making Small Talk

People often make small talk to start a conversation. The topics for small talk are general and impersonal, such as the weather, sports, a compliment, or a general comment about something the speakers have in common. Look at the following examples.

Expressions/Structures	Responses
Wonderful weather we're having!	Yes. It feels like spring.
What rotten weather!	I know. It's really snowing hard.
Nice day isn't it?	Yes, it's beautiful.
Are you enjoying the party?	Yes I am. The people are very nice.
Wasn't that hockey game great yesterday?	Yes. They are playing really well.
Are you new to the class?	Yes. I just registered yesterday.
That's a fabulous umbrella. Can I ask where you got it?	Thanks. There was a sale at Sears just last week.
Have you been waiting a long time?	No. Just a few minutes. I hope the bus is on time.

Speaking Activity 8

Work with a partner. Write YES if you think the following openers are appropriate and NO if you think they are not appropriate. Decide where you could use the appropriate openers.

Opener	Appropriate	Response	Location
Hot enough for you?	_____	_____	_____
Having a good time?	_____	_____	_____
What terrible weather we're having!	_____	_____	_____
Boy this elevator is slow!	_____	_____	_____
I heard about your divorce!	_____	_____	_____
Is the bus running on time?	_____	_____	_____
Are you a foreigner?	_____	_____	_____
Where do you live?	_____	_____	_____
You look different. Did you put on a lot of weight?	_____	_____	_____
Great dog! Is he a lot of trouble to look after?	_____	_____	_____
What a nice jacket! How much did you pay for it?	_____	_____	_____

Speaking Activity 9

Work with a partner. Think of openers and responses to use in the following situations. Then role-play a small talk conversation for the class. Ask the class to guess the situation.

1. You are waiting for the elevator.
2. You are waiting for your fitness class at the gym.

3. You are at a park.

4. You are at a party.

5. You are looking for a grammar book in a bookstore.

6. Other:

Communication Focus: Inviting

Extending Invitations

Would you like to . . .

I'm having some people over for pizza after school. Would you like to join us?

Do you feel like . . .

Are you hungry? Do you feel like going out for something to eat?

How about . . .

Are you doing anything on Saturday? How about going out to a movie?

Accepting

I'd love to.

That would be nice.

That's a great idea. I would really like to.

That sounds good.

Refusing and Making Excuses

I'm sorry, I can't. I have a dental appointment.

I'm afraid I can't. I have to study for an important test.

I would really like to, but I'm busy. My sister is coming over.

I'd love to, but I can't. I'm babysitting. Maybe we can get together some other time?

IS IT REALLY AN INVITATION?

Many English speakers will use expressions such as the following:

- Let's get together some time!
- Let's do lunch soon!
- Why don't we go out after school one of these days?
- Why don't you drop by sometime?
- We should have dinner soon.

These are **NOT** invitations. These are just expressions of liking and admiration. A true invitation must include a specific date and time.

Grammar Note: The Present Progressive Tense to Express Future Plans

In English, we use the present progressive tense for an action in progress.

Example

I am studying English now.

We also use the present progressive tense to express future plans. When we use the present progressive tense in this way, we need to have a future time reference in the sentence.

Examples

I am taking a vacation when this course ends.

What are you doing next summer?

They are going out tomorrow night.

 Please go to the website for more practice with this structure.

Speaking Activity 10

Walk around and invite a different person to four of the following activities which appeal to you. Other people will invite you to other activities. Respond honestly. Accept and turn down invitations.

Examples

I'm having some people over to play bridge tomorrow. Would you like to join us?

My friend and I are going swimming next Saturday. Do you feel like coming with us?

1. Go to a movie (choose a specific time and date)
2. Go shopping (choose a specific place)
3. Have dinner in a restaurant (choose a specific one)
4. Have coffee at a café (choose a specific one)
5. Go to a basketball game
6. Go to a museum
7. Go to a karaoke bar
8. Go for a walk (choose a specific place)
9. Go dancing
10. Go fishing
11. Go skating
12. Go hiking
13. Go to a play or concert

Communication Focus: Describing Personal Characteristics

We often use adjectives to describe people or things. Sometimes we use an example or an explanation to illustrate or strengthen the description.

Adjectives	Examples
outgoing	Sonia is outgoing. She is usually the life of the party.
quiet/shy/reserved	Jason is quiet, shy, and reserved. He doesn't like going to parties.
cautious	Paul is cautious. He always checks his answers.
ambitious	Michelle is ambitious. She wants to be the president of a banking company.
optimistic	Barack is optimistic. He never believes that anything bad will happen.
adventurous	Anita is adventurous. She always wants to go to new places and meet new people.
eager	Helen is eager to improve her English. She practises and studies all the time.
persistent	James is very persistent about finding a job. He sends out resumés all the time.
impulsive	Kim is impulsive. She frequently buys things on the spur of the moment, without thinking very long.
confident	Dave is very confident. He believes everyone wants to be his friend.
energetic	Linda is energetic. She does twice as much as anyone I know.

Speaking Activity 11

Use three adjectives to describe yourself, and explain why you chose them. Ask your partner for a description.

Adjectives That Describe Me

1. _____
2. _____
3. _____

Adjectives That Describe My Partner

1. _____
2. _____
3. _____

Speaking Activity 12

Answer the following questionnaire by yourself. Then share your answers with a partner and give reasons for your choices. Get together with another pair of students. What do you have in common? What are your differences?

Questionnaire

1. Are you a day person or a night person?
2. Are you a city person or a country person?
3. Are you an outgoing person or a shy person?
4. Are you an adventurous person or a cautious person?
5. Are you confident or are you sometimes unsure of yourself?
6. Are you an optimist or a pessimist?
7. Are you independent or do you need to do things with others?
8. Are you persistent or do you give up easily?
9. Are you an easy-going person or are you a tense person?
10. Are you systematic and organized or are you disorganized?
11. Are you a hard-working person or are you a lazy person?
12. Are you energetic or are you a low energy person?
13. Are you impulsive or do you plan everything?
14. Are you a risk taker or are you careful?
15. Are you a serious person or are you light-hearted?
16. Are you a doer or are you an observer?

Speaking Activity 13

Work in groups of four. Write down each other's favourite colours in order of preference. When you finish, use the information about colour preferences provided in the Answer Key to analyze everyone's personalities. Your partner will agree or disagree and give reasons.

Discuss what you think of analyzing personality through the use of colour preferences. Choose someone to report what your group learned.

Name	Favourite Colours	Agree/Disagree
_____	_____	_____
_____	_____	_____
_____	_____	_____
_____	_____	_____
_____	_____	_____
_____	_____	_____
_____	_____	_____
_____	_____	_____

Useful Expressions

Agreeing	**Disagreeing**
Yes, I agree.	I don't agree.
That's true.	I don't think so.
That's right.	Not really.
Absolutely!	You're wrong!
Right on!	No way!

Speaking Activity 14

Work with a partner to complete these colour expressions. What does each of these expressions mean? After completing the expressions, join the expression to its meaning.

Colour Expression	**Meaning**
To be as _____ as a ghost	to yell loudly
To be _____ with envy	very dark
To catch someone _____ handed	very suddenly
Out of the _____	catch someone in the act
To be black and _____	to go out on the town
To see _____	covered with bruises
To paint the town _____	to be very angry
The wild _____ yonder	to be very pale
As _____ as night	to be jealous
To scream _____ murder	far away over the horizon
To be _____ in the face	to be angry
To have _____ blood	to be royalty or aristocracy

Communication Focus: Complimenting

English speakers compliment each other frequently. Compliments are a good way to let someone know that you like or admire them and to start a conversation. The most frequently used adjectives in compliments are: great, nice, and good. Some other adjectives which we often use in compliments are: wonderful, terrific, fabulous, awesome, beautiful, and gorgeous.

Structure/ Expression	Examples	Responses
I like/love . . .	I love your new bag. Where did you get it?	Thank you. I bought it when I was on holiday.
. . . looks great . . .	That shirt looks great on you.	Thank you. It's kind of you to say that. I got this for my birthday.
. . . looks fantastic/ awesome/terrific . . .	That sweater looks terrific.	Thanks. Do you really like it?
What a nice . . .	What a nice skirt!	Thanks. My aunt made it for me.
You did a good (excellent) job . . .	You did a good job on this essay.	Thanks. It took a long time.
. . . is wonderful	Your haircut is wonderful!	Thank you.
. . . is incredible	Your English is incredible!	Thank you for saying that.
. . . is beautiful/ gorgeous/fabulous	Is that your couch? It's really gorgeous!	I'm glad you like it.

Speaking Activity 15

Work in groups of three. Take turns giving each other compliments on articles of clothing, possessions, or actions. With each compliment, ask a question to get more information. Continue until each person in the group has given and responded to two compliments.

Speaking Activity 16

Your instructor will borrow one item from each student in the class and put these into a bag or box and mix them up. Working in pairs, take two items out and develop a role-play using complimenting. Present your role-play to the class. Listen for compliments and responses.

Communication Focus: Handling Problems in Communication

Asking for Repetition or Clarification

Here are some expressions to use when you don't understand and you want the speaker to repeat or to rephrase the information in other words.

Expressions

Pardon me?
I beg your pardon?
Excuse me?

Could you please repeat that?
Pardon me, could you say that again, please?
I'm sorry, I didn't get that.
I'm sorry, I'm not following you.
Could you explain that again, please?
I am not sure I understand what you mean.
I'm sorry. I'm not sure what you mean. Did you say . . . ?

Expressions to Use If the Speaker is Speaking Too Quietly

Could you please speak up? I didn't catch that.
I'm sorry, I didn't hear what you said.

Expressions to Use If the Speaker is Speaking Too Quickly

Could you speak more slowly, please? I can't follow you.

Phrases to Check If the Listener Understands

Do you understand?
Is that clear?
Are you with me?
Are you following me?
OK so far?

SPEAKING STRATEGY

When you don't understand, don't feel nervous about asking the speaker to repeat as often as necessary.

Speaking Activity 17

What kind of language learner are you? Answer the following questionnaire by yourself. Then discuss your answers with a partner. Ask for clarification if you do not understand your partner's ideas. Report about your partner to the class.

Write YES next to the statements you agree with and explain why.

1. Learning a language means making a lot of mistakes.
2. Very intelligent people learn language much faster than others.
3. Learning a language means practising constantly.
4. Learning a language means learning rules.
5. Learning a language means learning how to become a better language learner.
6. Language learning is much easier if you are learning an important or exciting language.
7. Complete this sentence: Learning a language is like _____

Speaking Activity 18

Number the following items in order of importance starting with "1" as the most important, "2" as the second most important, etc.

The best ways to learn English are to . . .

☐ memorize vocabulary and expressions.

☐ speak as much as possible in class.

☐ analyze the language others are using.

☐ be brave. Don't be afraid to make mistakes.

- [ ] learn grammar rules.
- [ ] write out grammar exercises and English sentences.
- [ ] read as much as possible.
- [ ] ask the teacher to correct all your mistakes.
- [ ] listen to a lot of different kinds of material—movies, news, conversations.
- [ ] write down new words and make notes in class.
- [ ] forget about grammar. Relax and enjoy yourself.
- [ ] look for opportunities to practise speaking wherever you can.

Listening 2

Before You Listen

Pre-listening Vocabulary

1. You will hear these words and expressions in the listening selection.
Work with a partner or by yourself to write the correct vocabulary next to the
definition.

Vocabulary

hit the nail on the head	feel embarrassed	jump to conclusions
inhibited	give up	monitor
eager	figure out	in charge of
extrovert	hold on	characteristics

Definition	Vocabulary
qualities or features of someone or something	_____
prejudge, presume, presuppose	_____
check something, examine	_____
be exactly right	_____
outgoing, not reserved	_____
feel ashamed	_____
stop, quit	_____
enthusiastic, keen	_____
discover, solve	_____
in control of	_____
reserved, self conscious	_____
wait, be patient	_____

2. Work with a partner. You are going to hear an interview on the audio CD about good and poor language learners. Organize the following personality characteristics into the categories below.

eager to communicate
friendly and outgoing
shy
good guesser
tries everything to get the message
    across
embarrassed about making mistakes
extrovert
upset about mistakes

systematic
organized
in charge of their learning
create opportunities to use the
    language
pretend not to understand
nervous about speaking in a second
    language

Characteristics of Good Language Learners	Characteristics of Poor Language Learners	Characteristics You Are Not Sure About

 Listening for the Main Ideas

Listen to the interview once and answer these questions.

1. What is the relationship of the speakers?

2. Where are they?

3. What are they discussing?

LISTENING STRATEGY

If you can preview the vocabulary and ideas that you are going to hear, it will be easier for you to understand the message.

Listening Comprehension

Listen to the interview again. Mark these statements TRUE or FALSE according to what you hear the speakers say.

1. Good language learners use many different strategies.

2. Good language learners look for opportunities to use the language.

3. Good language learners avoid talking to strangers.

4. Good language learners try only one method to get their message across.

5. Good language learners will stop paying attention if they don't understand.

6. Good language learners are good at guessing meaning.

7. Good language learners get upset if they don't understand all the words.

8. Good language learners don't have to work very hard at learning a second language.

9. Good language learners are upset about making mistakes.

10. Good language learners plan time for studying and practising.

11. Good language learners experiment with different methods of learning.

12. Good language learners are not responsible for their learning.

13. Good language learners are very emotional.

Personalizing

Discuss the following questions with your partner.

1. Which good language learner strategies do you use? Which ones do you want to acquire?

2. How can you acquire these new strategies?

Speaking Activity 19

What kind of learner are you? Working on your own, write TRUE or FALSE after each statement. Then compare your answers with a partner and read the information in the answers box. What are some differences between you and your partner?

Question	T/F	My Partner
1. I always do my homework as soon as I can.		
2. I usually do my homework the night before it's due.		
3. I enjoy speaking English with others.		
4. I usually do better on grammar tests than in speaking with others.		
5. I rarely speak English to native speakers because they might not understand me.		
6. I enjoy watching English movies and TV programs, even if they are difficult to understand.		
7. I often ask other students questions and tell them my opinions.		
8. I often imagine myself speaking English in many different situations.		
9. The problem with conversation classes is that all the other students make mistakes when they speak.		
10. Your grammar needs to be very good before anyone can understand you.		
11. The teacher usually doesn't ask me to speak and that's why my speaking is poor.		
12. I hate making mistakes when I speak.		
13. I think the teaching of the teacher is the most important factor in how well we learn.		
14. I am only studying English because I need it for school and work.		
15. It's usually difficult to find words to express my ideas in English.		
16. I practise English wherever and whenever I can.		
17. I try to understand the feelings and attitudes of English speakers.		

Please check the Answer Key for the answers.

Pronunciation: Word Stress

Pronouncing English words can be tricky. This is because words in English come from many sources, including German, French, Latin, and Greek. In English, when words have more than one syllable, not all the syllables receive the same stress. One syllable is usually pronounced longer, louder, and with higher pitch. Stressing a syllable means that we pronounce the vowel in that syllable louder, longer, and with higher pitch.

In some English words, however, there is very predictable word stress. In this chapter we are going to examine some words with predictable stress.

 Pronunciation Activity 1

1. Listen to the speaker on the audio CD say these words, and underline the stressed syllable in each word. Check your answers with your partner. Can you figure out a rule for pronouncing these words? Afterwards, repeat the words after the speaker.

optimistic	conversation	attention	courageous
introduction	decision	curious	superstitious
energetic	opinion	opportunity	ambitious
characteristic	individual	individualistic	ability
communication	commercial	familiarity	originality
security	systematic	necessity	practical
enthusiastic	romantic	passion	comical
delicious	expression	comprehension	psychological
occupation	conclusion	grammatical	gorgeous

Please see the Answer Key for the pronunciation rule and the stressed syllables in the above words.

2. Work with a partner. Can you think of five other words with the same stress pattern? Share your answers with the class. Then, use as many of these words as you can to write a dialogue. Perform your dialogue for the class.

 Pronunciation Activity 2

Listen to the following words and underline the stressed syllable. Can you state the rule for stress placement? Afterwards, repeat the words after the speaker.

table	pumpkin	apron	scissors
button	garden	pocket	folder
handle	picture	blanket	carpet
lettuce	barrel	pillow	purpose
illness	zipper	jacket	kitchen
cousin	turkey	ceiling	

Please see the Answer Key for the rule and the stressed syllables in the above words.

Pronunciation Activity 3

Listen to the following words and underline the stressed syllable. Can you state the rule for stress placement? Afterwards, repeat the words after the speaker.

airport	armchair	toenail	backpack
driveway	ashtray	raincoat	sunglasses
greenhouse	bookstore	bluebird	blackbird
blackboard	classroom	doorbell	eyebrow
haircut	headache	bookcase	

Please see the Answer Key for the rule and the stressed syllables in the above words.

 Pronunciation Activity 4

Listen to the following words. Underline the stressed syllable. What is the rule for stress placement? Afterwards, repeat the words after the speaker.

escape	forget	attract	contain
admire	request	receive	decide
suggest	improve	conclude	improve
survive	surprise	respect	admit
offend	replace	protect	announce
forgive	arrest	repeat	

Please see the Answer Key for the rule and the stressed syllables in the above words.

 Pronunciation Activity 5

Listen to the following words and underline the stressed syllable. What is the rule for stress placement? Afterwards, repeat the words and sentences after the speaker.

Record: He kept a record.
Record: He recorded his voice.

Conduct: They conducted themselves very well.
Conduct: Their conduct was very good.

Produce: This country produces agricultural products.
Produce: They sell the extra produce to other countries.

Project: They worked hard on the project.
Project: The bank projected higher profits for the coming year.

Progress: They made great progress in learning English.
Progress: He progressed to the final stage.

Suspect: She suspected him of committing the crime.
Suspect: The police want to question the suspect.

Please see the Answer Key for the rule and the stressed syllables in the above words.

Pronunciation Activity 6

Listen to the words in each of the lists. Which word does not belong in the list?

ice cream	complain	backache	combine	mysterious
syrup	release	head band	destroy	millionaire
pepper	resume	today	delight	permission
winter	elect	ear ache	capture	anxiety
travel	summer	bracelet	devote	delicious
July	resign	earring	disturb	ambition

Word that does not belong:	Word that does not belong:	Word that does not belong:	Word that does not belong:	Word that does not belong:
_____	_____	_____	_____	_____

 Pronunciation Activity 7

Put the words in the following list into the correct category, according to the stress patterns. Then listen to the speaker say the words and check your answers. With two partners, use as many of the words as possible to make up dialogues.

	occasion/ ta**ta**ta	**com**pliment/**ta**tata	to**day**/ tata	**heart**ache/**ta**ta
tomorrow	_____	_____	_____	_____
beautiful	_____	_____	_____	_____
September	_____	_____	_____	_____
different	_____	_____	_____	_____
October	_____	_____	_____	_____
friendliness	_____	_____	_____	_____
fantastic	_____	_____	_____	_____
mistake	_____	_____	_____	_____
happiness	_____	_____	_____	_____
sorrow	_____	_____	_____	_____
confident	_____	_____	_____	_____
homework	_____	_____	_____	_____
breakdown	_____	_____	_____	_____
shoelace	_____	_____	_____	_____
awesome	_____	_____	_____	_____
jealous	_____	_____	_____	_____
believe	_____	_____	_____	_____
wristwatch	_____	_____	_____	_____
terrific	_____	_____	_____	_____
selfish	_____	_____	_____	_____
honest	_____	_____	_____	_____
restless	_____	_____	_____	_____
practical	_____	_____	_____	_____

	occasion/ tatata	compliment/tatata	today/ tata	heartache/tata
November	_____	_____	_____	_____
sincere	_____	_____	_____	_____
sorry	_____	_____	_____	_____
excellent	_____	_____	_____	_____
wonderful	_____	_____	_____	_____
competent	_____	_____	_____	_____
pessimist	_____	_____	_____	_____
cautious	_____	_____	_____	_____
optimist	_____	_____	_____	_____
bother	_____	_____	_____	_____
imagine	_____	_____	_____	_____

Communicating in the Real World

Try to use your English in your community. Working alone or with a partner, make up a questionnaire about language learning to administer to one or more native speakers in your school or your community. Write four to eight questions about language learning and show them to your teacher. When you find someone to interview, introduce yourself and find out information such as how many languages the person speaks, how he or she learned the languages, as well as other information. Report your findings to the class.

Self Evaluation

Rate yourself (using a scale of 0–5, where "5" is the highest ranking) and write your comments in each section of the chart. Show the chart to your teacher and discuss your strengths and weaknesses.

Topic	Good (5, 4)	Improving (3, 2)	Needs more work (1, 0)
Grammar and Language Functions 1. Introducing oneself 2. Talking about facts and habits using the simple present tense. 3. Introducing others 4. Using conversation openers 5. Inviting 6. Expressing future plans with the present progressive tense. 7. Describing personal characteristics 8. Complimenting 9. Handling problems in communication 10. Adjectives 11. Colours			

Topic	Good (5, 4)	Improving (3, 2)	Needs more work (1, 0)
Speaking Strategies 1. When introducing people, give some interesting information or point out something they have in common so that a conversation can begin. 2. When you don't understand, don't feel nervous about asking the speaker to repeat as often as necessary. 3. What other speaking strategies did you use?			
Listening Strategies 1. If you think about what you are going to hear, and try to predict what people will say, you can understand the conversation more easily. 2. If you can preview the vocabulary and ideas that you are going to hear, it will be easier for you to understand the message. 3. Evaluate your listening after each listening activity. Ask yourself how well you understood the main ideas. Don't be afraid to ask questions about points you did not understand very well. 4. What other listening strategies did you use?			
Pronunciation Word stress			

Vocabulary and Language Chunks

Write 10 sentences using vocabulary from the chapter.

1. _____
2. _____
3. _____
4. _____
5. _____
6. _____
7. _____
8. _____
9. _____
10. _____

My plan for practising is . . . _____

_____

_____

CHAPTER 2
Experiences and Achievements

Thinking and Talking

Work with a partner. Make up three or four categories to put these famous people into. Join another pair of students and compare your categories. What are some questions you would like to ask these people? Report the categories you used and the most interesting questions to the class.

John Lennon	Mao Tse Tung	Diego Maradona
Cleopatra	Yao Ming	Catherine the Great
George Washington	Bill Gates	Michael Jackson
George Clooney	Leonardo da Vinci	Avril Lavigne
Barack Obama	Brad Pitt	Jackie Chan
Nelson Mandela	Elvis Presley	Pablo Picasso
Angelina Jolie	Lance Armstrong	Alexander Graham Bell

Listening 1

Before You Listen

Pre-listening Vocabulary

1. You will hear a conversation on the audio CD that includes the following words and expressions. Work with a partner or by yourself and write the correct vocabulary items next to the definitions.

Vocabulary

ancestor	achievement	pension
scholarship	to enrol	discrimination
research	to recruit	vehicle
huge	widow	radiation
to accomplish	award	
literacy	doctorate	

Definition	Vocabulary
to do something, to achieve something	_____
person from whom another person is descended, a predecessor	_____
money to pay school expenses, a special prize for outstanding students	_____
very large	_____
prize	_____
a woman whose husband is dead	_____
a means of transportation such as an automobile	_____
to register as a student	_____
something important which is done/completed	_____
energy given off by uranium which can be converted to power and which can cause damage to people exposed to it	_____
to take on people as workers, students, or members	_____
prejudice, unfairness, bias	_____
income/money for people unable to work	_____
ability to read and write	_____
organized study, investigation	_____
highest university degree	_____

2. Work with a partner. You are going to listen to a conversation about Michelle Obama and Marie Curie. Think about what you already know about these two women and what you would like to learn about them.

	What We Know	**What We Would Like to Learn**
Michelle Obama		
Marie Curie		

Listening for the Main Ideas

Listen to the interview on the audio CD and answer these questions.

1. Why are Laura and Lindsay discussing Michelle Obama and Marie Curie?

2. Which woman does Laura admire the most at first? Why?

3. Who does Lindsay admire? Why?

Listening Comprehension

Listen to the interview again. As you listen, number the events in the order in which they are mentioned.

Michelle Obama

☐ Michelle Obama was born and raised in Chicago.

☐ Michelle joined the Chicago law firm of Sidley & Austin, where she later met Barack Obama.

☐ Michelle Obama's ancestors were slaves.

☐ Michelle went to Harvard Law School.

☐ Michelle studied sociology and African American studies at Princeton University.

☐ Michelle became vice president of community and external affairs for the University of Chicago Medical Center.

☐ Michelle ran literacy programs. She recruited African American students for Harvard.

Marie Curie

☐ Marie Curie received the first advanced scientific research degree, or doctorate, to be awarded to a woman in France.

☐ Marie worked as a physics professor at a girls' school and she continued her research.

☐ Marie, her husband Pierre, and another researcher, received the Nobel Prize for Chemistry.

☐ Marie Curie enrolled at the Sorbonne, a famous university in Paris. She graduated in first place in physics.

☐ Marie Curie was the first woman to hold a chair at the Sorbonne.

☐ Marie established the Curie Foundation in 1920 to work on medical applications for radium.

☐ Marie Curie helped fit ambulances with portable x-ray equipment for medical purposes.

Personalizing

Work in groups of four. Decide as a group which woman you would choose to name a scholarship after. Give two reasons to support your decision.

 LISTENING STRATEGY

Listen for signals which tell you the order in which things happened. Listening for words like *first, then, after that,* and *finally* will help you to understand the sequence of events or the times when actions happened in the past.

Vocabulary and Language Chunks

Write the number of the expression next to the meaning. After checking your answers, choose six expressions and write your own sentences.

Expressions

1. chair of a committee
2. a sad ending
3. to win hands down
4. at a loss
5. to turn down
6. to set up
7. to be in your shoes
8. true calling
9. you have got to be kidding
10. community service
11. external affairs
12. to rise above
13. to make a decision

Meanings

☐	to refuse
☐	to win easily
☐	uncertain about what to say or do
☐	the person in charge of a committee
☐	most suitable job or profession
☐	to be in your position
☐	to decide
☐	an unhappy end
☐	to handle or overcome something difficult or painful
☐	you are not serious
☐	unpaid work which helps people in the community
☐	matters dealing with outside businesses or organizations
☐	to put in place, establish

Communication Focus: Talking about Past Experiences, Narrating

Structures/Expressions	Examples
Once when I . . .	Once when I was walking home late in the evening, I saw a ghost.
What happened was . . .	What happened was that one of my neighbours was playing a trick on some friends because it was Halloween.
I remember when . . .	I remember when I first saw him in his costume, I screamed.
I'll never forget the time . . .	I'll never forget the time that I was so scared I couldn't move.

Here are some questions we can ask when talking about past events.

Questions/Conversation Stimulators

What happened when . . .

Tell me about the time . . .

What did you do when . . .

How did you feel when . . .

Tell me about what happened next?

What happened after that?

When we retell past events in chronological order (the order in which they happened), we often use sequence markers or signals to make the time of the events clear.

Sequence Markers/Time Signals

First/first of all/to begin with

Then/next/after that/at that time/at that point

Finally/in the end

Grammar Note

When we talk about a completed action in the past, we use the simple past tense.

Affirmative	Negative	Interrogative
Jane lost her passport last year.	She didn't lose her purse.	Did she lose anything else?
Ricardo watched a movie last night.	He didn't watch the news.	Did he watch the football game too?
Larry was at work yesterday.	He wasn't at home.	Was Maria at work too?

Note that we often use the simple past tense to make polite offers or to ask what someone prefers.

Examples

Did you want more coffee? (A server asking a customer)

Did you need your receipt? (A cashier asking a customer)

Would you like more coffee? (*Would you like* is also very often used to make offers)

Grammar Note

When we talk about an action that was in progress at a specific point in the past we use the past progressive tense.

Affirmative	Negative	Interrogative
Jane was travelling in China last May.	She wasn't travelling alone.	Was she travelling on a visitor's visa?
They were using computers at 10:30 this morning.	They weren't using the camera equipment.	Were they using the Internet?

 Please go to the website for more practice with this structure.

SPEAKING STRATEGY

Use signals such as *then*, *after that*, and *finally*, to make it easier for listeners to understand when events happened.

Speaking Activity 1

Work with a partner. Read the following story. There are some missing sentences in the story. Insert the sentences from the chart below into the appropriate blanks. Then, with your partner, tell the story in a few sentences. The students who can tell the whole story in the fewest sentences win!

The Story of Romeo and Juliet, Star-crossed Lovers

Romeo's family and Juliet's family were enemies. _____ . The Prince of Verona stopped the fighting and said that any more battles would be punished by death. _____ . Romeo was very depressed about this situation. Juliet was only 13 years old at that time, but Count Paris fell in love with her and asked for her hand in marriage. Juliet's family planned a ball, at which her mother wanted Juliet to accept the count's marriage offer. _____ . Romeo attended the ball in disguise but instead of Rosaline, he met and fell in love with Juliet. _____ . When they saw each other, Romeo and Juliet declared their love and promised to marry. _____ . After their secret marriage, Romeo was challenged to a fight by Juliet's cousin, Tybalt, but he refused because he knew that Tybalt was now his cousin too. Because Romeo refused to fight, Mercutio, Romeo's best friend, decided to fight in his place._____. When Romeo heard about Mercutio's death, he was upset and so he fought and killed Tybalt in revenge. _____ . At the same time, Juliet's family was pressuring her to marry Count Paris. _____ . She got a special drug from Friar Lawrence, who felt sorry for her. This special drug would make her appear lifeless for two days and then she would wake up. _____ . Juliet took the drug, appeared to die, and was put into the family tomb. _____ . Romeo was extremely upset about Juliet's death and bought poison to kill himself. _____. Romeo attacked the count and killed him. He then took the poison and died. _____ . The two families were so sad when they found their children dead that they finally agreed to end their violent fighting.

1. Romeo went to Juliet's tomb where he saw the Count Paris, who had wanted to marry Juliet.

2. Juliet asked Friar Lawrence to send a messenger to tell Romeo about her plan.

3. After that, the Prince of Verona exiled Romeo.

4. At that point, Juliet awoke from her drugged sleep and when she found Romeo dead she stabbed herself with his knife because she didn't want to live without him.

5. The next day, they were married by Friar Lawrence who hoped that Romeo's and Juliet's marriage would stop the fighting between the two families.

6. When Romeo's friends found out about his sadness, they convinced him to attend the ball at Juliet's home because they thought that Rosaline would be there.

7. During the fight, Tybalt killed Mercutio.

8. After the ball, Romeo secretly went up to Juliet's balcony and heard her talking about her love for him, even though their families were enemies.

9. Before he met Juliet, Romeo was very much in love with Rosaline, a young woman who didn't love him.

10. At the beginning of the play, the families were fighting each other in the streets of Verona.

11. Meanwhile, Romeo's servant told him that he heard that Juliet was dead.

12. At that point, Juliet decided that the only solution was to die or to look as if she died.

Speaking Activity 2

Work with a partner. Tell your partner about an interesting movie or TV program that you saw recently. Use sequence markers or signals to tell the story. Your partner will report to the class.

Speaking Activity 3

Work in groups of three. Individually, choose one of these topics to talk about. Use time expressions and sequence markers such as *first, next, then,* and *after that*. Other students will ask questions as you tell your story. When everyone has finished, report about the most unusual information you found out.

Topics

- The first time I fell in love
- My first trip
- An important event in my life
- My greatest accomplishment so far
- My first day in this country/city
- The happiest day of my life

Communication Focus: Encouraging Conversation

One way to keep a conversation going is to ask open-ended questions. These are different from YES/NO questions (closed questions). A YES/NO question only requires "yes" or "no" as an answer and the conversation may end. An open-ended question begins with a question word and encourages conversation because the other person will give more information, which can lead to more questions and information.

YES/NO Questions (Closed Questions)

Are you a student?
Did you drive to work?
Do you like to travel?
Did you study English before?
Do you like this course?

Questions that begin with a question word but require very specific answers are also closed questions.

Where are you from?
How old are you?
What language do you speak?

Open-Ended Questions

Why are you studying at this school?
How did you feel when you first came here?
What do you want to do in your life??
Why did you decide to study English?
How do you like this course?

Speaking Activity 4

Work with a partner. Each of you will choose a topic of your own. Make a statement about your topic. Your partner will ask as many questions as possible for two minutes. Answer your partner's questions. Then reverse roles. When you finish, change partners and start again.

Topics

- My dream job
- The last time I went to a restaurant/party/movie
- A good experience
- The strangest thing I have ever seen
- What I want to do in my life
- My first day here
- My favourite pastime

Speaking Activity 5

This is a story-and-question game. Work in groups of four. Choose one person to start and decide the order of speakers. The first person will choose a topic from the following list and will talk about it for two minutes. The other people in the group will ask questions which the speaker has to answer. The point is to interrupt and stop the speaker from finishing his or her story. If the speaker finishes the story, or if the group runs out of questions, then the speaker scores a point. If the speaker has not finished the story or if the group is still asking questions when the two minutes are up, the speaker does not get a point. The next speaker then takes a turn. The teacher will tell you when to start.

Topics

- The person I admire the most
- A movie I saw
- My last vacation
- My first love
- My hero
- An important person in history
- My favourite place

Communication Focus: Describing Past Habits

We use *used to + the base form of the verb* to talk about habitual actions or states in the past which are no longer true. We also use *would* to talk about habitual actions in the past, but not about states.

Examples

I *used to live* in a small town and I *would ride* my bicycle everywhere.
(I don't live in a small town and ride my bicycle everywhere anymore.)

I *didn't use to speak* English very well and I *would make* many mistakes.
(I speak English well and don't make many mistakes now.)

Did Andrea *use to live* in an apartment building?
(She doesn't live in an apartment building now.)

Ellen and Sherry *didn't use to take* art classes.
(They take art classes now.)

 Please go to the website for more practice with this structure.

Speaking Activity 6

Work in groups of three. Find out the following information from each person in your group and then choose someone to report some interesting facts to the class. Remember to ask open-ended questions to keep your conversations going.

Question	Partner #1	Partner #2
What did you use to look like as a teenager?	_____	_____
Where did you use to live?	_____	_____
What did you use to do in your free time?	_____	_____
What problems did you use to have?	_____	_____
What used to make you happy at that time?	_____	_____
What used to be important to you when you were younger?	_____	_____
Describe the friends you use to have then.	_____	_____
What did you use to dream of doing?	_____	_____
What didn't you use to do that you do now?	_____	_____

Speaking Activity 7

Work with a partner. Read this article about women. Replace the verbs with *used to* or *would*. Then discuss some differences between you and your grandmother, using *used to* or *would*.

Life has changed a great deal for women in North America in the past 100 years. In the early 1900s, daily life *was* completely different for women. Women *didn't have* the right to vote. Most women *were* housewives and home makers. Most women *stayed* home and *took* care of children. Women *were* responsible for all the housework. Women *washed* clothes by hand and they *cooked* meals from scratch. There was discrimination against women in many professions. Most women *didn't get* very much education. Women didn't *compete* in the Olympics. There *were* no women pilots or sports figures. Thank goodness things have changed. Women are much better off today and they don't want life to be the way it *was* 100 years ago.

Communication Focus: Explaining

When we give explanations, we often talk about the causes or the results of an event. We use transition words or logical connectors to make the relationships between the ideas clear.

Stating Reasons

We can state reasons by using logical connectors such as *because, because of, since,* and *due to*.

Examples

My favourite singer is Avril Lavigne *because (since)* she has a great voice.

Avril Lavigne is my favourite singer *because of (due to)* her great voice.

We can also state reasons by using expressions such as *the explanation for . . . is . . .* and *the reason why . . . .*

Examples

The explanation for her popularity lies in her great voice.

The reason why she is so popular is her great singing voice.

Stating Results

We can use logical connectors to state results, such as *so, therefore,* and *as a result*.

Examples

Madonna is a great performer so she is very popular.

Madonna is a wonderful singer; therefore, she is very popular.

Madonna is a fantastic performer, and as a result, she is very popular.

 Please go to the website for more practice with this structure.

Speaking Activity 8

Work with a small group. Discuss the reasons for and results of these events. Present your ideas to the class.

Event	Reasons	Results
The dinosaurs disappeared from the earth.	_____	_____
The ice age ended.	_____	_____
The earth has gotten warmer.	_____	_____
Man landed on and explored the moon.	_____	_____
Bill Gates developed an operating system for computers.	_____	_____
The US government developed the Internet in the latter part of the twentieth century.	_____	_____
Social networking websites are extremely popular.	_____	_____

Listening 2

Before You Listen

Where are these places? Do you know any other famous tourist attractions?

Work with a small group. Look at the following list of countries. Decide which five are the most visited countries in the world.

Japan	Australia	United States
Turkey	Spain	Italy
China	Mexico	Egypt
Thailand	France	Greece

1. _____   4. _____

2. _____   5. _____

3. _____

Pre-listening Vocabulary

You will hear these words and expressions used on the audio CD for the following activity. Work with a partner or by yourself and write the correct vocabulary items next to the definitions.

Vocabulary

attraction	incredible	to rank
magnificent	master	impress
doubt	memories	fascinating
resort	skyscrapers	to roam
to glisten	ancient	cruise
to marvel	monument	

Definition	Vocabulary
a trip by boat	_____
to give a rating or position	_____
beyond belief, amazing	_____
to be full of amazement and wonder	_____
uncertainty, questioning	_____
wander around	_____
to affect/to please greatly	_____
famous or historical building, statue, or structure	_____
very old, from the distant past	_____
very tall buildings	_____
thing or place that attracts tourists	_____
interesting, captivating, appealing	_____
a vacation place where people stay	_____
exceptional, beautiful	_____
to have a shiny surface	_____
recollections, what you remember	_____

 Listening for the Main Ideas

After you listen to the material for the first time, answer these questions.

1. What kind of listening text is this?

2. What is the purpose of it?

3. What are the two main things which the speaker discusses?

Listening Comprehension

As you listen to the text for the second time, answer the following questions.

LISTENING STRATEGY

Listening for numbers and for signal words which tell the order of something (for example, *first, second,* and *third*) will help you understand details.

1. What was the most-visited country in the world and how many tourists went there?

2. What were some things people did in France?

3. What did Paris look like?

4. What was the second-most visited country and how many tourists went there?

5. What did people do there?

6. What was the third-most visited country? How many tourists did it receive?

7. What was the fourth-most visited country? How many visitors did it receive? What did people do there?

8. What was the fifth-most visited country? How many visitors did it get?

9. Write in the rank (first, second, third, etc.) in terms of the number of visitors to the following tourist attractions.

   ☐ Trafalgar Square

   ☐ Notre Dame Cathedral

   ☐ Tokyo Disneyland

   ☐ Disneyland Paris

   ☐ Times Square

   ☐ Niagara Falls, Ontario, Canada

10. Fill in the missing information in the following sentences.

   a) Times Square in _____ got _____ visitors.

   b) The National Mall and Memorial Parks in _____ had _____ visits.

   c) Walt Disney World's Magic Kingdom in _____ had _____ visits.

   d) Trafalgar Square in _____ got _____ visitors.

   e) Fisherman's Wharf in _____ had _____ visitors

   f) The Notre Dame Cathedral in _____ had _____ visitors.

Personalizing

Discuss the following with a partner.

1. Have you visited any of these places?

2. Which places would you like to visit? Explain why.

3. Why do you think people enjoy travelling?

Vocabulary and Language Chunks

Write the number of the expression next to the meaning. After checking your answers, choose six expressions and write your own sentences.

Expressions	Meanings
1. to have no doubt	☐ to visit special sights
2. to go sightseeing	☐ to remembers things when one returns home
3. to take home memories	☐ to spend time dancing
4. to go dancing	☐ to travel by boat
5. to take a cruise	☐ to be the place where something is located
6. well worth visiting	☐ the best time is now
7. to come second	☐ at the same time in the same place
8. ever a better time	☐ a place tourists visit
9. same time, same place	☐ to be second, third, etc.
10. tourist attraction	☐ to be sure
11. to be home to	☐ to take pictures
12. to take photographs	☐ to spend time swimming
13. to go swimming	☐ important and beneficial to visit

Communication Focus: Talking about Similarities and Differences

Structures/Expressions	Examples
similar to . . .	Travelling in North America is similar to travelling in Europe.
the same as . . .	Travelling in the US is the same as travelling in Canada.
as . . . as . . .	Trains are as comfortable as planes.
different from . . .	Travelling by bus is different from travelling by car.

> *Grammar Note: Comparative and Superlative Forms*
>
> We can use comparative and superlative forms of adjectives and adverbs to talk about similarities and differences.
>
> To form comparative forms of short (one-syllable) adjectives and adverbs add *–er* to the adjective or adverb.
>
> To form superlative forms of adjectives and adverbs add *–est* to the adjective or adverb.
>
> When the adjective or adverb ends in *–y*, replace the *y* with *i* and add *–er* or *–est*.

Comparative Forms

Canada is bigger than France.

Mexicans seem happier than Canadians.

Superlative Forms

Russia is the biggest country in the world.

I think Mexicans are the happiest people in North America.

With adjectives and adverbs of two or more syllables, we use *more/less . . . than* for comparative forms and *the most . . . the least . . .* for superlative forms.

Comparative Forms

I think Paris is more beautiful than Los Angeles.

New York is more exciting than Chicago.

Buenos Aires is busier than Cordoba.

Superlative Forms

Paris is the most beautiful city in the world.

New York is the most exciting city in North America.

Buenos Aires is the busiest city in Argentina.

We can also use *more/less, less/fewer,* and *the least/the fewest/the most* with nouns.

Travelling is more fun than staying at home.

Staying home costs less money than travelling.

France had the most tourists in 2007.

We had the fewest problems travelling in the US.

North Americans have the least time to travel.

Irregular Forms

Examples

Are you a *good* traveller? Yes, but my sister *is better*. She's *the best* traveller in the family.

Is the weather in London *bad* in winter? Yes, it's *worse* than the weather in Rome. London has *the worst* weather in Europe.

 Please go to the website for more practice with this structure.

Speaking Activity 9

Interview your partner. Report the most interesting answers to the class.

Question	Partner's Response
1. Describe the best vacation you had.	_____
2. What is your idea of a perfect vacation?	_____
3. What do you like doing the most on vacation?	_____
4. What countries have you visited? Compare two of them.	_____
5. What cities have you visited? Compare two of these.	_____
6. What is your favourite city or country to visit?	_____
7. What is most important to you when you are travelling in a new city?	_____
8. What is the most convenient thing to have on a trip?	_____
9. What is the most memorable trip you have taken?	_____
10. What do you like the least about travelling?	_____

Speaking Activity 10

Work in groups. Make as many comparisons as you can about the following topics. The teacher will give you a certain period of time. At the end of this time, the group with the most comparisons wins!

1. Staying home/travelling
2. Travelling in this country/travelling in foreign countries
3. Camping/staying in hotels
4. Plane travel/train travel
5. Taking a cruise/taking a driving holiday
6. Hiking/cycling
7. A vacation in the country/a city vacation
8. Visiting museums and monuments/visiting the countryside
9. Visiting ancient places/visiting modern cities and areas
10. Vacationing at a beach/vacationing in the mountains

SPEAKING STRATEGY

Control your nervousness and your emotions when you are speaking. Don't be afraid to ask for help from others when you have problems expressing your ideas.

Speaking Activity 11

Work with a partner. Make as many comparisons as you can about the following topics.

1. Tourists/travellers
2. Man-made tourist attractions/natural sites that people visit
3. Men/women
4. Teenagers/adults
5. Teachers/students

Communication Focus: Paraphrasing

When we paraphrase we explain the same idea in different and usually simpler words.

Original Sentence	Paraphrase
He intended to purchase an exquisite gift for his beloved.	He planned to buy a nice present for his sweetheart.
He concluded, after much deliberation, that it was inappropriate.	He decided, after thinking it over, that it was not the right thing to do.
Travel brings out the best and the worst traits in human beings.	When they travel, people can do very good and very bad things.

Speaking Activity 12

Work with a partner to paraphrase the following proverbs.

Proverb	Paraphrase
You can lead a horse to water but you can't make him drink.	_____
All that glitters is not gold.	_____
A stitch in time saves nine.	_____
The early bird catches the worm.	_____
Heaven helps those who help themselves.	_____
Rome was not built in a day.	_____
When in Rome, do as the Romans.	_____
Birds of a feather flock together.	_____
You can't judge a book by its cover.	_____

Can you think of other proverbs? If so, add them to the list and paraphrase them.

SPEAKING STRATEGY

When you don't know or can't think of a word, look for different ways to express the idea. Use synonyms or paraphrase.

Speaking Activity 13

Look at the list of words. Check off the ones you know. Move around the class and ask other people to explain the words you don't know until you have an explanation of all the words.

adventure	atmosphere	grove
boulevard	vehicle	night life
glacier	unique	metropolis
disembark	surrounding	remote
leisurely	byways	landscape

Speaking Activity 14

Work in groups of three. Good news! You and your group have just won an all-expenses-paid trip to one of the following places. You need to agree on the place that you will visit. Discuss the advantages and disadvantages of the trip, and the reasons for your choice. Present this information to the rest of the class.

Adventure 1

Patagonia, Glacier Adventure: You start your adventure in Buenos Aires, the capital of Argentina. Spend six nights in a five-star hotel in this European-style city with wide boulevards and an exciting night life. Then take a four-day cruise of Patagonia to see glaciers and fiords—one of the most dramatic landscapes in the Americas. Explore Punta Arenas—see elephant seals and penguins. See Cape Horn with its forests and the Perito Moreno glacier, where you will see and hear blocks of ice breaking free and crashing into the sea. Visit Ushuaia, the world's most southern city. Finally, disembark in Santiago, a modern metropolis surrounded by snow-capped mountains before you fly back to Buenos Aires. What's included? Accommodation, cruise, hotels, most meals, transfers—14 days.

Adventure 2

India and the Taj Mahal: There is no better way to appreciate village life in Rajasthan, Northern India than by cycling and camel riding. Start off by spending two days in Delhi. Then, go by train to northern India. We combine cycling and camel riding with visits to famous palaces and forts. We start off in the desert, and our camel caravan takes us to remote villages and forts. After three days of riding, we visit the walled cities of Jaisalmer, Jodhpur, and the Pink City of Jaipur before starting our cycle ride. Our cycle ride is leisurely, so that we can absorb the atmosphere, culture, and scenery. If you haven't cycled since your school days, don't worry. The roads are flat, the days are relaxed, and we have a backup vehicle for your convenience. We finish by watching the sun rise at the Taj Mahal. Afterwards, there will be train transportation back to Delhi. What's included? Accommodation in good hotels, all meals, camels, bicycles, all transfers, and train travel—15 days.

Adventure 3

Africa Adventure: Imagine seeing the plains of Tanzania from the top of Africa's highest mountain—Mount Kilimanjaro. East Africa's amazing parks and its highest mountain are included in this unique vacation. You get the incredible chance to experience hiking to the top of Mt Kilimanjaro and through Masai country in search of wildlife. Combining the walks with wild animal viewing is a unique East African experience. What's included? All meals, all transfers, all national park and conservation fees, one night four-star hotel accommodation in Nairobi, four nights accommodation at a three-star hotel, safari-style tents, and all group camping and catering equipment, including a supply vehicle—16 days.

Adventure 4

Cycling Vietnam: Riding a mountain bike along the highways and byways of Vietnam is one of the most rewarding ways to experience this country. Travelling the same way as the locals do lets you interact with the many Vietnamese people you will meet on this adventure. We explore peaceful highlands, palm-lined beaches, and country roads that lead through mango and coconut groves. Along our route you will be in contact with the real Vietnam—an experience you will find hard to forget. What's included? English-speaking tour leader, group medical kit, all hotel accommodations, all meals, airport transfers, all group transport including the train from Hanoi to Hue in AC soft sleeper carriage, domestic flight to Ho Chi Minh City, use of a mountain bicycle, and sightseeing excursions—15 days.

Adventure 5

The Middle East: A fascinating introduction to some of the most magnificent highlights of the Middle East. On this tour you will wander through the bazaars of Damascus and discover hidden courtyards and busy marketplaces. You will shop in Aleppo and appreciate the Roman influence in Palmyra. While in Jordan, enjoy a swim in the Dead Sea, count the stars in the desert skies, and be amazed by the ancient city of Petra. In Egypt, climb Mount Sinai at sunrise, snorkel in the Red Sea, and experience the madness that is Cairo, Africa's largest city. All this in just two weeks! Visit Syria, Jordan, and Egypt. What's included? Fully escorted tour with a tour leader and driver, all activities, sightseeing and entrance fees, all meals, camping/hotel accommodations, all transport and transfers—15 days.

Speaking Activity 15

Work with a group. Research and plan the trip of a lifetime—the most exciting and memorable trip a person can take. Make a poster about your trip. Give descriptions of the activities and places you will visit. Make a presentation about your trip to the class. The class will vote for the best trip.

Pronunciation: Regular Past Tense Endings

The pronunciation of the regular past tense ending *–ed* differs depending on the verb.

In some verbs the past tense ending is pronounced /d/. For example, played, called, and tried.

In some verbs the ending is pronounced /t/. For example, kicked, washed, and danced.

In some verbs the ending is pronounced /Id/. For example, wanted, needed, painted, and seeded.

 Pronunciation Activity 1

Listen to the speaker say these verbs and write the correct pronunciation of the past tense as /t/, /d/, or /Id/. Afterwards, pronounce the words after the speaker.

cooked _____	prayed _____	punished _____
looked _____	shopped _____	wanted _____
washed _____	hoped _____	attended _____
finished _____	lived _____	decided _____
competed _____	enjoyed _____	pressured _____
played _____	voted _____	asked _____
changed _____	killed _____	planned _____
waited _____	discriminated _____	refused _____
stayed _____	promised _____	

 Pronunciation Activity 2

The following exercises will help you understand the rule for the pronunciation of the regular past tense endings.

1. Listen to these verbs and write the pronunciation of the past tense ending. What is the rule for the pronunciation of the past tense of these verbs? Afterwards, repeat the verbs after the speaker.

needed	invited
wanted	added
started	visited
ended	decided

2. Listen to these verbs and write the pronunciation of the past tense ending. What is the rule for the pronunciation of the past tense of these verbs? Afterwards, repeat the verbs after the speaker.

washed	bumped	helped	tripped
laughed	watched	coughed	punched
fished	finished	danced	dressed
liked	stuffed	ranked	
talked	stopped	hiked	

3. Listen to these verbs and write the pronunciation of the past tense ending. What is the rule for the pronunciation of the past tense of these verbs? Afterwards, repeat the verbs after the speaker.

lived	rained	viewed	cried
closed	roamed	showed	starred
wandered	called	smiled	cycled
tried	played	answered	

Check the Answer Key for the pronunciation rules.

Pronunciation Activity 3

Say these sentences to a partner and then listen to the speaker on the audio CD. Were your sentences correct?

1. She turned down the marriage proposal.
2. They travelled on a cruise ship.
3. Mary Anne started off skiing on the lowest hills.
4. Man landed on the moon ages ago.
5. Ali stayed at home last summer.
6. The students biked along the paths in the park.
7. We shopped in the best stores.
8. Tom climbed up to the top of the mountain.
9. They called off their travel plans.
10. Anna looked up the prices of the flights.

Pronunciation Activity 4

Work in small groups. Tell each other three things that you did in the past in your free time using the following list of verbs. Two of the statements you make should be true and one should be false. People can guess which one is false. The person who guesses correctly scores a point.

visit	shop	dance	invite
sail	enjoy	try	amuse
act	ski	contact	play
decide	hike	stay	paint
travel	call up	bike	view
walk	snorkel	watch	discover

Pronunciation Activity 5

Work in groups of four. Make up a story using the following verbs in the past tense. The first person will choose a verb and make a statement. The second person chooses another verb and makes a statement that follows the first sentence. Continue until you have used at least 10 verbs. The group which finishes first and recites their story without making mistakes wins.

relax	celebrate	attend
start	watch	smile
hike	invite	stop
cycle	show	plan
view	visit	punish
call	refuse	pressure
help	kill	travel
laugh	hope	climb
stuff	decide	camp
wash	enjoy	stay
cry	pray	experience
dance	promise	

Pronunciation Activity 6

Work with a partner. Adventurous Alexa and Shy Sandra are classmates. Tell what each of them did last year. Make as many sentences as you can by choosing from the lists below and by adding your ideas.

Actions	**Time Expressions**
stay home	most weekends
hike with friends	almost every weekend
talk to new people	every day
plan to go out every day	as often as possible
listen to music by herself	during the winter
watch videos alone in her apartment	in the evenings
walk in the park	once in a while
clean the apartment	frequently
talk to herself	daily
learn to ski	usually
travel to new cities	seldom
date new people	occasionally
call up classmates	almost never
visit friends	whenever she could
try to meet new people	always
like to have fun	often
taste new foods	

Communicating in the Real World

Try to use your English to talk to people outside your classroom. Working either on your own or with a partner make up a questionnaire about what this city and life in the city used to be like. You could ask questions about the following things: size, transportation, stores and plazas, and services. Write four to eight questions and show them to the teacher. Then, interview people outside your class. Report what you learned to the class.

Self Evaluation

Rate yourself (using a scale of 0–5, where "5" is the highest ranking) and write your comments in each section of the chart. Show the chart to your teacher and discuss your strengths and weaknesses.

Topic	Good (5, 4)	Improving (3, 2)	Needs more work (1, 0)
Grammar and Language Functions 1. Narrating, talking about past events using the past tense and past progressive tense 2. Encouraging conversation 3. Describing past habits with *used to* 4. Explaining 5. Discussing similarities and differences 6. Paraphrasing			
Speaking Strategies 1. Use signals such as *then, after that,* and *finally* to make it easier for the listener to understand when events happened. 2. Control your nervousness and your emotions. Don't be afraid to ask for help from others when you have problems expressing your ideas. 3. When you don't know or can't think of a word, look for different ways to express the idea. Use synonyms or paraphrase. 4. What other speaking strategies did you use?			
Listening Strategies 1. Listen for signals (*first, then, after that*) which tell you the order in which things happened. 2. Listening for numbers and signal words like *second* or *third* will help you understand details. 3. What other listening strategies did you use?			

Topic	Good (5, 4)	Improving (3, 2)	Needs more work (1, 0)
Pronunciation Past tense endings			

Vocabulary and Language Chunks
Write 10 sentences using vocabulary from the chapter.

1. _____
2. _____
3. _____
4. _____
5. _____
6. _____
7. _____
8. _____
9. _____
10. _____

My plan for practising is . . . _____
_____
_____
_____

Thinking and Talking

Discuss the following questions with a group.

1. Do you think friendship is important? Why?
2. What is your definition of friendship?
3. How important are friends to you? Please explain.

Listening 1

Before You Listen

Pre-listening Vocabulary

1. You will hear these words and expressions in the lecture. Work with a partner or by yourself and write the correct vocabulary items next to the definitions.

Vocabulary

relationship	aggressive	resource	to imitate
peer	to influence	emotional	effect
social	to function	security	collaboration
cognitive	benefit	researcher	cooperative

Definition	Vocabulary
a person who is the equal of another person in position or age	_____
result	_____
connection between people and their behaviour and feelings towards each other	_____
to copy, mimic, be like	_____
relating to society and people	_____
action of working together	_____
having to do with thinking or using reasoning	_____
able to work with others	_____
advantage, good result	_____
a person who studies or investigates	_____
a source or supply of help	_____
likely to attack or do harm	_____
to have the power to change or affect	_____
relating to feelings or emotions	_____
to serve as	_____
safety, feeling of safety	_____

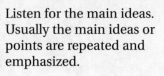

LISTENING STRATEGY

Listen for the main ideas. Usually the main ideas or points are repeated and emphasized.

2. Work with a partner. You are going to hear a lecture on the audio CD about how friendship affects children and adults. What do you think the lecturer will say? Make three predictions.

a) _____

b) _____

c) _____

Listening for the Main Ideas

Listen to the interview once and answer the following questions.

1. Why are children's friendships and relationships important?

2. What do children learn from relationships and friendships?

3. Were any of your predictions correct?

🎧 Listening Comprehension

1. Listen to the interview again. The following are some sentences from the interview. As you listen, number the sentences in the order in which the lecturer mentions them.

☐ First of all, friendships serve as emotional resources, both for having fun and for dealing with stress.

☐ Secondly, let's look at friends as cognitive resources. Children teach one another in many situations and are usually very good and effective in this activity.

☐ As emotional resources, friendships give children security.

☐ The basics of friendship—close relationships and common interests—are first understood by children in early childhood.

☐ It's true friendships and close relationships may lead to better social development, but, perhaps, well-adjusted children are just better at making friends.

2. Listen to the interview again. Mark these statements TRUE or FALSE according to what you hear the speakers say.

a) The best predictors of how well people will do in their lives are how they behaved in the classroom and their marks.

b) Friendships can help children and teenagers deal with the stress of family breakdown or failure in school.

c) Children learn from each other in only one way.

d) Friendships help children develop social skills.

e) Children fight more often with their friends than with non-friends.

f) The lecturer is sure that having friends leads to better social development.

Personalizing

Work in groups of four. Read the following quotation by Helen Keller. She was deaf and mute, and overcame her disability to become a famous teacher to the deaf.

> My friends have made the story of my life. In a thousand ways they have turned my limitations into beautiful privileges, and enabled me to walk serene and happy . . . .
>
> —Helen Keller

1. What do you think Helen Keller means by this?

2. Do you agree with her feelings about friendship?

3. Discuss what you have learned from your friends.

Vocabulary and Language Chunks

Write the number of the expression next to the meaning. After checking your answers, choose six expressions and write your own sentences.

Expressions	Meanings
1. have friends	☐ have the same interests
2. get along with	☐ to be like the others in the group
3. have an influence on	☐ resolve differences
4. spend time	☐ spend as much time as needed
5. have fun	☐ enjoy oneself
6. care about each other	☐ pass the time
7. solve problems	☐ feel affection and concern for each other
8. deal with stress	☐ eliminate difficulties
9. take time	☐ manage emotional or physical pressure
10. work out differences	☐ have an effect on
11. fit in with the group	☐ like and work well with
12. share interests	☐ have relationships with people who like you

Communication Focus: Requesting

English speakers make requests in three main ways:

1. Commands or imperatives: These can sound rude or angry depending on the tone of voice. Using please helps to soften the request.

Example

Close the door.

Please close the door.

2. Requests using modals (could/would): These modals are considered more polite that can/will. There are two types of requests using modals.

a) Direct requests: Could/Would you lend me your notes?

b) Indirect questions: I was wondering if you wouldn't mind lending me your notes?

If people think the request is a lot to ask, they will use a longer, indirect request.

Example

Would it be at all possible for me to borrow your car tomorrow afternoon?

3. Hints: There is no stated request in these situations. People understand from the context what the request is.

Examples

It's very hot in here! (This could be a request to open the window.)

Is that the doorbell? (This could be a request to answer the door.)

Are there any cookies left? (This could be a request for a cookie.)

Communication Focus: Making Requests for Permission

Structures/Expressions	Examples	Responses
May I . . . ?	May I use your dictionary?	Go ahead/Sure.
Could I . . . Can I . . .	Can I borrow $10?	I'm sorry, I can't lend you the money. I'm broke.
Is it all right . . . ? Is it OK if . . . ?	Is it OK if I open the window?	No problem.

Making General Requests

Structures/Expressions	Examples
Can you . . .	Can you spell your name please?
Will you . . .	Will you please take a message for John?
Could you . . .*	Could you tell me the time, please?
Would you . . .*	Would you ask James to call me, please?
Could/would you do me a favour . . .*	Could you do me a favour? Would you let me borrow your notes from yesterday's class?
Could you possibly . . .*	Could you possibly pick up the newspaper when you are at the store? I need it for my next class and I don't have time to get it myself. (The speaker regards this as an imposition and gives an explanation to soften the request.)

* These requests are more formal.

Grammar Note: Modals Can, Will, Could, Would

The modals *can, will, could,* and *would* are followed by the base form of the verb without *to* or an *–ing* ending.

However, *would you mind* requires the *–ing* ending (gerund) form of the verb.

Some Responses to Requests

Positive	Negative
No problem.	Sorry, I can't . . .
Sure.	No, sorry.
Of course.*	I'm afraid not.*
Certainly.*	Sorry but . . .
I'd be glad to.*	I'd rather not.*
With pleasure.*	I'm afraid that's impossible.*
OK.	I don't think so.
	Maybe another time.
	It's not a good idea because . . .
	Are you kidding?

*These responses are a little more formal sounding.

Speaking Activity 1

Work with a partner. Make a list of five requests you could make to a friend and five requests you could make to an acquaintance. Choose the appropriate forms. Then practise requesting and responding. Do you notice any differences between requests in North America and requests in your country?

Requests to a close friend

1. _____
2. _____
3. _____
4. _____
5. _____

Requests to an acquaintance

1. _____
2. _____
3. _____
4. _____
5. _____

Communication Focus: Making General Requests for Information

Structures/Expressions	Examples
Can you tell me . . .	Can you tell me what friendship means to you?
Could you tell me . . .	Could you tell me how many Canadian friends you have?
I'd like to know . . .	I'd like to know if you are on Facebook?
Would you mind telling me . . .	Would you mind telling me what your email address is?
Please tell me . . .	Please tell me what your friend's name is.
Do you know . . .	

Grammar Note: Indirect Questions

We can use direct and indirect questions when making requests for information. Direct questions use interrogative structures and word order.

Indirect questions often seem more polite and formal. They do not use interrogative structures and word order. Indirect questions are introduced by a phrase such as: *Could you tell me, please tell me,* and *I'd like to know . . . .*

Direct Questions	Indirect Questions
What kind of people do you like?	I'd like to know what kind of people you like.
When did you come to this school?	Please tell me when you came to this school.
Have you ever met a famous person?	Could you tell me if you have ever met a famous person?
What is your favourite place to go with friends?	Can you tell me what your favourite place to go with friends is?
Is friendship important to you?	Would you mind telling me if friendship is important to you?
Where does your best friend live?	Can you tell me where your best friend lives?
How often do you get together with friends?	I'd like to know how often you get together with friends.

Indirect questions/statements with *I don't know* are very common in conversation.

Examples

I don't know what you're talking about.
I don't know why we're having problems.
I don't know where he lives.

 Please go to the website for more practice with this structure.

SPEAKING STRATEGY

When the listener doesn't understand or is having trouble following you, giving an example can sometimes be helpful.

Speaking Activity 2

Keep a record of the requests you make in the next week. Record three requests you make in the following locations. Bring your log to school and compare it with your partner's.

Location	Who Did You Make the Request To?	What Actual Words Did You Use?	What Was the Response to Your Request?	Was Your Request Successful? Why?
A store/business				
At school				
In your neighbourhood				

Speaking Activity 3

Work with a partner. The following dialogues are not in order. Please try to organize them so that they make up logical request dialogues. Then, practise saying the dialogues

1.

☐ James: Could you tell me how much the ticket is?

☐ James: Could you please tell me where track three is?

☐ James: Could you please tell me how to get to Burlington.

☐ James: Would you happen to know when the next train is?

☐ James: Two tickets please. Would you have change for a fifty?

☐ Ticket agent: Certainly. You walk through the underpass and then you will see the sign for track three.

☐ Ticket agent: It's $5.00 for adults.

☐ Ticket agent: Sure, no problem.

☐ Ticket agent: You need to buy a ticket and take the train on track three.

☐ Ticket agent: The next one leaves at 4 o'clock.

2.

☐ Joe: What is it?

☐ Joe: Not at all. Of course I'll drive you home.

☐ Joe: Hi Felipa, how's it going?

☐ Joe: Felipa, I was wondering if you are free after school and if you could help me with my presentation. Your English is so much better than mine.

☐ Felipa: I don't have any plans after school and I would be happy to give you a hand. There's just one thing.

☐ Felipa: If I stay after school, I'll miss my ride. Would you mind giving me a drive home after we finish working?

☐ Felipa: Just great. No complaints.

Speaking Activity 4

Work with a partner. Some of the following statements are requests, and others are responses to requests. Complete the dialogues by writing a response or a request, as required.

Example: a) Could you possibly lend me $20 until tomorrow?

b) <u>Sure, no problem</u>

1. a) Would you mind moving to another desk? I can't see the presentation from here.

b) _____

2. a) Would you be so kind as to tell me the time?

b) _____

3. a) May I borrow your notes on the weekend? I missed class last Wednesday.

   b) _____

4. a) I'd like to know if you wouldn't mind looking after my cat this weekend. I am going out of town.

   b) _____

5. a) It's really warm in this room!

   b) _____

6. a) _____

   b) Unfortunately, I don't have one.

7. a) _____

   b) Sure go ahead. No problem.

8. a) _____

   b) I'm afraid not. I need mine.

9. a) _____

   b) Of course!

10. a) _____

   b) I would really like to, but I won't be able to.

Speaking Activity 5

Work with a partner. Choose the best answer to each of the following questions. Explain why you didn't choose the other response.

1. What would a teacher say to her students?
   a) Would you mind terribly handing in your assignments next Thursday?
   b) Please hand in your assignments next Thursday.

2. What would you say to your neighbour?
   a) I'm going away next week. Keep an eye on my place.
   b) Would you mind keeping an eye on my place while I'm away next week?

3. What would a student say to a teacher?
   a) My assignment's not finished. Can I have more time?
   b) I would appreciate it if you could give me an extension for my assignment. I haven't been able to finish it yet.

4. What would your roommate say to you?
   a) I need help hanging up this picture.
   b) Could you please give me a hand hanging up this picture?

5. What would a boyfriend say to a girlfriend?
   a) Why is this place such a terrible mess? My parents are coming over.
   b) Would you mind helping me clean up my place?

6. What would you say to the librarian at your school?
   a) Could I renew these books please?
   b) Could I possibly trouble you to renew these books?

7. What would a passenger say to a taxi driver?
   a) I'd like to get off at the next street please.
   b) Stop at the next street.

8. What would a guest say to the hostess?
   a) Would you mind telling me where the bathroom is?
   b) Have you got a bathroom here?

9. What would you say to an acquaintance?
   a) Could I possibly have your email address? I'd like to send you some information.
   b) What's your email?

10. What would you say to a stranger?
    a) Excuse me, would you happen to have the time?
    b) What time is it?

SPEAKING STRATEGY

If we think the request we are making is a lot to ask (a big imposition), then we generally use longer, more elaborate requests, and often give an explanation.

Speaking Activity 6

1. Would you make these requests to an acquaintance, a friend, or a stranger? Restate them, if possible, for the other two categories.

Request	To an Acquaintance	To a Friend	To a Stranger
Could you please tell me the time?	OK	What's the time? What time do you have?	Excuse me, would you happen to have the time?
Would you be kind enough to change seats with me?			
Can you give me your phone number?			
Could you possibly move aside? I can't see.			
Can you give me a lift home?			
Would you be good enough to put these in the mail?			
Tell me about your first kiss.			
Can you lend me $200?			

Speaking Activity 7

Work in pairs. Use indirect questions to find out the answers to the following questions.

Example

What are the names of your two best friends?

> Question: Could you tell me what the names of your two best friends are?

> Answers:

> a) _____

> b) _____

1. Where do your friends live?

    Question:

    Answers:

    a) _____

    b) _____

2. What do they do for a living?

    Question:

    Answers:

    a) _____

    b) _____

3. What are they like?

    Question:

    Answers:

    a) _____

    b) _____

4. Where and when did you meet?

    Question:

    Answers:

    a) _____

    b) _____

5. What things do you like to do together?

    Question:

    Answers:

    a) _____

    b) _____

Speaking Activity 8

The following is a list of some of the qualities of a friend. Talk about friendship with your partner and decide together what you consider to be the five most important qualities in a best friend. Report your decisions to the class and give explanations.

outgoing	kind	strong
friendly	trustworthy	stubborn
easy-going	happy	secretive
intelligent	romantic	energetic
funny	good-looking	independent
loyal	serious	confident
a good listener	optimistic	adventurous
interesting	enthusiastic	

Communication Focus: Asking for and Giving Information about Actions that Started in the Past

We use the present perfect continuous tense to describe actions that started in the past and are still true at the moment of speaking. We use the present perfect continuous tense to talk about how long an action has been going on.

Examples

Samantha moved to Florida in 2009. She still lives in Florida.
Samantha has been living in Florida since 2009.

Erica started driving to work in 2010.
Erica has been driving to work since 2010.

The Kims started speaking English when they moved to Toronto many years ago. They still speak English.
The Kims have been speaking English for many years (since they moved to Toronto).

Grammar Note

We use *for* or *since* when talking about how long an action has been continuing. *For* tells the listener how long the action has continued: for ten years, for three weeks, for a month. *Since* tells the listener when the action began: since 2010, since last month, since Monday.

We form the present perfect continuous by using *have been/has been + VERB + ing.*

Examples

Janet and Elena *have been smoking* for a few years.
I *have been studying* English for a long time.
My friend Pierre *has been living* in Ottawa since September.

 Please go to the website for more practice with this structure.

Speaking Activity 9

Work in groups of three. Find out how long each of you have been doing the following actions.

Actions	Me	Partner #1	Partner #2
Living in this city	_____	_____	_____
Studying at this school	_____	_____	_____
Speaking English	_____	_____	_____
Driving	_____	_____	_____
Playing (any) sports	_____	_____	_____
Doing any activity (for example: yoga, gardening, smoking, chewing your nails, etc.)	_____	_____	_____

Speaking Activity 10

Walk around and talk to at least eight classmates. Find out and record the following information. Report what you have discovered to the class.

Name	What's Your Favourite Pastime?	How Long Have You Been Doing It?

Communication Focus: Getting Time to Think

Often we need time to think about the answers before we can respond to a question. It's important to let the other person know that you plan to answer, but that you need some time to think. You can use some of these expressions—separately or together—to pause and organize your thoughts.

Hmm…	Let's see…	OK.
Ahh…	Let me think…	OK, well, let's see…
Well…	That's a good question.	

Speaking Activity 11

Using the following questions, interview your partner about his or her ideas on friendship and people.

1. Is it easy for you to make friends? Why or why not?

2. Do your friends have any characteristics in common?

3. Do you have any heroes or heroines, people that you admire and look up to? Why do you admire them?

4. In what ways do your friends influence you? Who has influenced you the most in your life?

5. Can you forgive and forget if someone hurts you? What would make you stop being friends with someone?

6. Why do you think some people enjoy having friends and being with people while others prefer being alone? Which category do you belong to?

7. What do you expect from your friends?

8. What is the most important thing in friendship?

9. Who do you prefer to spend time with—your friends or your family?

Speaking Activity 12

Working in groups of three, practise changing the direct questions below into indirect questions. Then interview each other using the newly formed indirect questions. Report three differences between you and your partners to the class.

Questions	Partner #1	Partner #2
What is your full name?		
What are some differences between names here and names in your country?		
Does your name have a special meaning? Why did your parents give you this name?		
How many people were there in your family when you were growing up? What are the differences between families here and in your country?		
What is your happiest childhood memory?		
What was your family life like when you were a teenager? What did you disagree with your parents about?		
How often and on what occasions does your family get together?		
Who is the head of the household in your family?		
What is the ideal family?		
Is family as important today as it used to be?		

Speaking Activity 13

Work in groups. Choose one of the topics below and write down points about the topic in order to tell the others. Use the suggested questions below the topic to get started, but you can also add more information. When you are ready, tell your story. The other students will interrupt you using indirect questions.

1. A sports event you watched or participated in: Who won?/What happened?/Who was playing?/Where was it?/How did you feel?

2. A recent purchase: What was it?/Why did you buy it?/What do you like about it?/What are you going to do with it?

3. A night out, a social event, or a party you attended: What was the purpose?/Who did you go with?/Who was there?/How did you get there?/Where was it?/What happened?

4. A movie, play, or TV program you saw recently: What was it about?/Who were the main characters?/What happened?/How did you like it?/What did you learn?

Speaking Activity 14

Work in groups of three. In the following list, the requests and responses are mixed up. Identify all of the requests and write them in the chart. Then write the matching responses for each request. Put + next to those expressions that you think are more formal and – next to the ones you think are informal.

Excuse me, would you happen to have change for a twenty?

Could you tell me what that is?

Speaking.

Could I speak to Natalie?

Would you mind my taking this seat?

Can I give you a shout tomorrow?

Could you run that by me again? What did you ask?

I'm sorry, I didn't catch that. What did you say?

Could you do me a favour?

Certainly. Will two tens do?

Nope, sorry.

Not at all. Please sit down.

ure, no problem.

I asked what day it was.

I'm sorry, but I don't have one.

I said the test's tomorrow.

I'd be glad to. What do you want me to do?

Got change for a five?

It's a stapler.

May I borrow your eraser?

Go ahead. I won't be using it for a while.

Could you possibly let me use your cellphone? I have an urgent call to make.

Requests

Excuse me, would you happen to have change for a twenty?

_____
_____
_____
_____
_____
_____
_____
_____

Responses

Certainly, will two tens do?

_____
_____
_____
_____
_____
_____
_____

Listening 2

Before You Listen

Pre-listening Vocabulary

1. You will hear these words and expressions on the audio CD. Work either with a partner or by yourself and write the correct vocabulary items next to the definitions.

household	portrait	caregiver
surpass	step child	newsworthy
breadwinner	adopt	release
legalize	outnumber	single parent
statistics	couple	census
data	poverty	

Definition	Vocabulary
person who earns most of the money in a family	_____
interesting enough to be in the news	_____
condition of being poor, having little or no money or means of support	_____
two people who are together in a relationship, usually a man and a woman	_____
to have more numbers of something	_____
a picture, a painting of a person	_____
to make legal by changing the law	_____
collection of numerical information	_____

Definition	Vocabulary
information in the form of facts and figures	_____
to make information available to the public	_____
spouse's child, not a biological child, as one's own	_____
to raise a child who is not a biological child	_____
to go beyond, to go above in numbers	_____
people who live together as a family	_____
a family with only one parent	_____
person who looks after others in a family	_____
an official enumeration or counting of a population	_____

Pre-listening Activity

In 2006, there were 8,896,840 families in Canada. This is a pie chart representing the total number of families in Canada. The different areas of the chart show **married**, **single-parent**, and **common-law families**. Which section do you think represents families with married couples? Which section represents single-parent families? Which section represents common-law families?

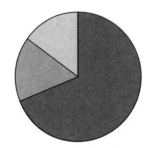

Check the answer key to find the answer.

Work with a partner to complete the following table. What do you know about families in Canada? What are some questions that you have about families in Canada?

What We Know about Families in Canada	Questions about Families in Canada
_____	_____
_____	_____
_____	_____
_____	_____

Listening for the Main Ideas

Listen to the interview on the audio CD once and answer these questions.

1. What is the main topic of this interview?
2. Were your guesses about the percentages of married-couple, single-parent, and common-law families correct?
3. Why are the speakers discussing this information?

LISTENING STRATEGY

When you examine what you already know about a topic, your background knowledge, you will find the listening easier to understand.

Listening Comprehension

Listen to the interview again and fill in the numbers related to the topics on the chart below.

Topic	Numbers
The year of the census	_____
The percentage of unmarried people over age 15	_____
The year the census began in Canada	_____
The percentage of families headed by married couples	_____
The percentage of couples without children	_____
The percentage of couples with children	_____
The year in which same-sex marriage was legalized	_____
The number of same-sex couples in Canada	_____
The percentage of married same-sex couples	_____
Same-sex couples make up what percentage of all couples?	_____
The percentage of families with children headed by a single parent	_____
The percentage of single-parent families headed by men	_____
The percentage of single-parent families in 1931	_____
The median family income for single-parent families in 2005	_____

Listen to the interview again and finish the following sentences from the recording.

1. Statistics Canada calls this information its _____.

2. It is based on data collected about Canada's _____, their living arrangements, and _____.

3. Statistics Canada uses the term "families" to define three types of households: _____, _____, and _____.

4. Surprisingly enough, even people in their 60s _____.

5. The census, for the first time, _____.

6. In the past, parents were left widowed because of _____.

7. Divorce rates and the fact that it is not considered wrong or shocking _____ single-parent families now.

8. Financial struggles _____.

LISTENING STRATEGY

Monitor your understanding. What parts of the listening did you have trouble with?

Personalizing

1. What is your reaction to the information you heard?

2. What surprised you the most?

3. What do you think the families of the future will look like?

Vocabulary and Language Chunks

Write the number of the expression next to the meaning. After checking your answers, choose six expressions and write your own sentences.

Expressions	Meaning
1. give us a snapshot	☐ people whose children have grown up and left home
2. give (some of) the highlights	☐ length of time people are expected to live
3. to be in the minority	☐ born to people who are not married
4. empty nesters	☐ finally, the right time
5. draw attention	☐ at the top of
6. breakthrough	☐ time is over
7. make up	☐ problems with money, finances
8. at the head of	☐ attract attention
9. it's about time	☐ constitute, amount to
10. born out of wedlock	☐ an event that removes a barrier to progress
11. life expectancy rates	☐ to be part of a group which makes up less than 50 per cent, to be smaller in number
12. financial struggles	☐ tell us about some of the most important parts
13. time is up	☐ give a picture

Communication Focus: Expressing Necessity in the Present and Future

Structures/Expressions	Examples
It's necessary to . . .*	It's necessary to pay tuition fees. (You have no choice. You must do it.)
I must . . .*	I must pay tuition fees.
I have to . . .**	I have to pay tuition fees.
I have got to . . .	I have got to pay tuition fees.

* used mostly in written or formal English
**used very often in conversation

Lack of Necessity

It isn't necessary to . . .	It isn't necessary to bring a gift.
He doesn't have to . . .	He doesn't have to work on Friday.
We don't have to . . .	We don't have to pay rent.

Question Forms

Is it necessary to . . .	Is it necessary to pay for the card?
Does he have to . . .	Does he have to take medicine?
Do we have to . . .	Do we have to sign a contract?

Communication Focus: Expressing Necessity in the Past

Structures/Expressions	Examples
It was necessary to . . .	It was necessary to pay tuition fees. (You had no choice. You did it.)
I had to . . .	I had to pay tuition fees.

Lack of Necessity

It wasn't necessary to . . .	It wasn't necessary to bring a gift.
He didn't have to . . .	He didn't have to work last Friday.

Question Forms

Was it necessary to . . .	Was it necessary to pay for the card?
Did he/we have to . . .	Did he have to take medicine?

Speaking Activity 15

Work with a partner. Discuss three things you have to do and three things you don't have to do when you live with your family. Then make up a list of things you had to do when you were a child and things you didn't have to do.

Living with Your Family

Things You Have To Do

_____

_____

_____

Things You Don't Have To Do

_____

_____

_____

When You Were a Child

Things You Had To Do

_____

_____

_____

Things You Didn't Have To Do

_____

_____

_____

Speaking Activity 16

Work with a partner. Tell your partner about four things you had to do before you came to this country. Try to use _first_, _next_, _then_, and _finally_ in your answers.

Before Coming Here

Me

_____

_____

_____

My Partner

_____

_____

_____

Speaking Activity 17

Read the following paragraph and the blog entry. Then list some advantages and disadvantages of living with a roommate. Compare your answers with a partner.

In North America, many young people leave home as soon as they have jobs and can afford to support themselves. Some leave home before they finish their schooling because they have to attend college or university in a different city. Young people want to be independent from their parents. They want to set up their own households, decorate according to their tastes, and live by their own rules. In some cases when they can't afford to pay all the expenses of living on their own, they have to look for roommates to share the costs. Sharing an apartment or a house with a roommate can be an interesting, rewarding experience or it can lead to serious problems. One thing is certain—young people have to learn to express their feelings, and they have to communicate and compromise to get along in these situations. Here is a blog entry about someone called "the roommate from hell"!

My roommate from hell made potatoes every day for dinner. Oh, but *how* did she make them? She put potatoes and water in a pan, and put the burner on the highest setting. After the water boiled over, and coated the burner with a sticky, slimy mess, she used to turn it down so that mess hardened on the stove. Then she would take her meal into the living room and plunk herself in front of the TV and slurp loudly as she ate. After eating, she rinsed her dishes and the saucepan in cold water (no soap), and put them back in the cupboard. And that was the ONLY cleaning she ever did. She used to borrow my food, my clothes, my beer, and I would never see these items again. And if I said anything, she would explode. She had a terrible temper. She used to call my friends awful names. Piles of clothing, books, and garbage used to litter the apartment we shared. I finally couldn't take any more and moved out!

Having a Roommate

Advantages	Disadvantages
_____	_____
_____	_____
_____	_____
_____	_____

Speaking Activity 18

Work in groups of three. Check off what your partners have to do and don't have to do in the places where they live. Report to the class.

Actions	Partner #1	Partner #2
Pay the rent	_____	_____
Share the kitchen	_____	_____
Pay utilities	_____	_____
Sign a lease	_____	_____
Take out the garbage	_____	_____
Be quiet	_____	_____
Clean up	_____	_____
Pay for Internet and cable TV	_____	_____
Shovel snow	_____	_____
Vacuum	_____	_____
Other	_____	_____

Communication Focus: Asking For and Giving Instructions, Describing a Process

Asking For Information

Structures/Expressions	Examples
Can/could you explain . . .	Could you explain how to fill in the form?
How can I . . . ?	How can I open the safe?
Do you know how to . . .	Do you know how to set the burglar alarm?
Please show me how to . . .	Please show me how to program the thermostat.
How does . . . work?	How does this appliance work?

Describing a Process

When we describe a process we often use sequence markers to clearly outline the steps and the order in which they occur.

Sequence Markers	Examples: Making a Snowman
First	First, you have to pack snow into a snowball. Make the ball bigger by rolling it in the snow on the ground until the ball is big enough to be the base for your snowman. Put the base on the spot where you want the snowman to stand.
Then	Then, make the middle section by repeating the first step, but the ball should be slightly smaller. Place the middle ball on top of the base.
Next	Next, repeat step one to make the snowman's head. This ball has to be smaller than the other two. Place the third ball on top of the middle section.
After that	After that, make the snowman's eyes by putting two pieces of charcoal on the head. Use a carrot for his nose. Cut small dots out of fabric and use this to form a mouth. Put a scarf or tie around the snowman's neck.
	Put sticks into the middle section for arms and put mittens on the ends of the sticks. Finish the snowman by adding a hat.
Finally, at the end	Finally, make your snowman special. Put some interesting clothes on your snowman or add some props, like skis, a broom or shovel, or some stuffed animals. Make your snowman a character.

Speaking Activity 19

Work with a partner. Read the following instructions for removing ink from clothing. How many steps are there? What are they? What are the sequence markers?

How to Remove Black Ink from a Garment

First, spray the stain with hairspray. Let it sit for a while and then try to sponge the ink out. If that does not work, try rubbing alcohol next. Put alcohol on the stain and sponge it off. As a last resort, try milk. After that, wash according to instructions. The stain should be gone.

Choose three of the following topics and describe the steps necessary to complete the task.

1. How to address an envelope
2. How to fill a bicycle tire with air
3. How to make an omelette
4. How to make friends
5. How to improve your English

Speaking Activity 20

Work with a partner. Number the steps in this recipe for chocolate chip cookies in the correct order. Explain what needs to be done first, after that, next, and so on.

Then join another pair of students. Check your recipes and together decide on a new process (a recipe or another task) that you are going to describe to your classmates. Then present your process to the class.

☐ Add flour mixture to batter and stir until combined.

☐ Drop small amounts of dough onto buttered cookie sheet.

☐ In a large bowl, mix together the two kinds of sugar and the butter for about two minutes. Beat in eggs, vanilla, water, until the batter is smooth.

☐ Preheat oven to 350°F.

☐ Bake in the oven for 8–10 minutes, or until lightly browned. Cool.

☐ Mix flour with baking soda and salt in medium bowl.

☐ Assemble these ingredients:

1 cup butter
1 cup brown sugar
1/2 cup granulated sugar
2 eggs
1 teaspoon each of vanilla and water

2 cups all purpose flour
1 teaspoon baking soda
1/2 teaspoon salt
2 cups chocolate chips (mixture of white and dark, if desired)

Pronunciation: Intonation Patterns for Questions and Statements

Intonation is the rising and falling of the pitch of the voice when we are speaking. Intonation patterns are important in English because they carry meaning. Intonation patterns tell the listener if the speaker has finished speaking or if the speaker is expecting an answer. Intonation carries as much meaning as vocabulary or grammar.

Rising intonation tells the listener that the speaker is asking a question and is waiting for an answer.

Are you still hungry?

Rising–falling intonation tells the listener that the speaker has finished.

I have never visited New York.

Common Intonation Patterns

1. **YES/NO Questions: Rising** intonation is used when people are uncertain, or when they are asking questions. YES/NO questions take rising intonation. The pitch of the voice rises on the last stressed syllable of the sentence.

Were they happy?

Could I borrow your dictionary?

2. **Statements and Commands:** Statements have a **rising–falling** intonation. Rising–falling intonation tells the listener that the speaker has finished speaking. In rising–falling intonation, the voice rises on the last stressed syllable of the sentence and then falls to its lowest pitch level.

They conducted a survey.

The children went to the movie.

Please leave the room.

Please sit down.

Please take the books with you.

3. **WH Questions:** We use **rising–falling** intonation with WH questions which begin with *what, where, when, why, how*. Indirect questions or information questions also take rising–falling intonation

Where are you going?

When will you be finished?

Please tell me where you live.

Could you tell me where John is.

4. We can use WH questions to ask someone to repeat, to ask for clarification or to express surprise. The intonation starts to go up on the question word and rises at the end of the question.

I'm looking for a new roommate.

What did you say?

Georgette moved out.

What?

We can use rising intonation to ask for confirmation.

First, I turn off the alarm, then I unlock the door. Right?

 Pronunciation Activity 1

Listen to the intonation patterns in this conversation. Decide if it is rising or falling intonation that you hear in each sentence in the conversation. Check your answers with a partner and the teacher.

Utterance	Rising	Falling
A. Front desk?	_____	_____
B. Wake up call, please.	_____	_____
A. What time?	_____	_____
B. Quarter past six.	_____	_____
A. Six?	_____	_____
B. Quarter past six.	_____	_____
A: OK	_____	_____

 Pronunciation Activity 2

Mark the intonation on these short sentences as you listen to them. Use rising arrows for YES/NO questions and falling arrows for final rising–falling intonation. Check your answers with a partner. Then arrange the sentences into a conversation and practise saying it.

1. I'm still hungry.

2. What do you feel like?

3. Take as many as you want.

4. You're welcome.

5. Where are they?

6. Are there any cupcakes left?

7. In the fridge.

8. I'm starving.

9. How many can I have?

10. Tons.

11. What?

12. Thanks.

Pronunciation Activity 3

Listen to the speaker and repeat these sentences. Then practise saying them with a partner.

1. What are the benefits of friendships?

2. What do we get from them?

3. I was wondering if I could borrow your notes?

4. What time is it?

5. Could you tell me how much the ticket costs?

6. Friendships provide children with ways of developing basic social skills.

7. Can I renew these books?

8. Did you learn a lot about relationships?

9. Could I talk to you for a moment?

10. Is anything wrong?

11. Do you have change for a twenty?

12. What did you say?

 Pronunciation Activity 4

Look at the following sentences taken from the listening exercise. Predict what the intonation patterns are. Draw intonation contours or arrows for rising or rising–falling intonation. Use correct punctuation in the sentences. Then listen to the sentences. Were you correct? Repeat the sentences after the speaker.

1. I think you will find these latest statistics very interesting.

2. Would you mind giving us some of the highlights?

3. Do you know what the definition of a child is?

4. Could you explain why that is?

5. Are you certain about that?

6. I wonder if it is because there are more divorces in that age group now.

7. Baby boomers are now finding themselves to be empty nesters.

8. I don't know if that is good for the country.

9. Don't you think we need more children, especially in a country like Canada?

10. Could you tell us how many same-sex couples there are in Canada?

11. What other information did we get?

12. Is there anything that surprised you?

Pronunciation Activity 5

Work with a partner. Ask each other four YES/NO questions and four WH questions. Listen to make sure your partner is using the right intonation.

Pronunciation Activity 6

Work in groups of four. Brainstorm a list of questions about friends, family, or housing that you could ask the other people in your class. When you have a list, each person will choose three different questions. Write out your sentences and draw intonation contours, and practise asking your questions. Walk around and ask as many people as possible. Report to the class.

Pronunciation Activity 7

This is a recipe for a favourite snack: roasted almonds. Read the recipe to a partner who will write down the steps. Use expressions for checking confirmation such as "Right" and "OK". Then write out your own recipe for something good to eat and tell your partner the steps. Read your partner's recipe to the class. The class will vote for the tastiest food.

What you need:

3-1/2 cups (875 mL) almonds, (1 lb/500 g)
1 tbsp (15 mL) extra virgin olive oil
2 tsp (10 mL) coarse sea salt
1-1/2 tsp (7 mL) smoked hot or mild paprika

What you do:

First, line a baking sheet with foil or parchment.
Next, in a large bowl, toss almonds with salt, oil, and paprika.
Then, spread evenly on baking sheet.
Finally, roast in 325°F oven for about 20 minutes, until lightly toasted, and
  then cool.

Communicating in the Real World

Try to use the language you have learned out in the real world. Work with a partner and make up a list of four to eight questions about family, friends, or relationships to ask people out in the community. Practise your questions and use appropriate intonation. Have a conversation with five people who are not in your class. Ask them the questions and record their answers. Report the most interesting information to the class.

Self Evaluation

Rate yourself (using a scale of 0–5, where "5" is the highest ranking) and write your comments in each section of the chart. Show the chart to your teacher and discuss your strengths and weaknesses.

Topic	Good (5, 4)	Improving (3, 2)	Needs more work (1, 0)
Grammar and Language Functions 1. Making requests 2. Indirect questions 3. Expressing necessity 4. Giving yourself time to think 5. Asking for and giving information about actions that started in the past			
Speaking Strategies 1. Requesting 2. General requests for information: indirect questions 3. Asking for and giving information about actions that started in the past 4. Getting time to think 5. Expressing necessity 6. Asking for and giving instructions; describing a process			
Listening Strategies 1. Listen for main ideas. The main ideas or points are usually repeated and emphasized. 2. Examine your background knowledge. 3. Monitor your understanding. What parts of the listening did you have trouble with? 4. What other listening strategies did you use?			
Pronunciation Intonation in statements and questions			

Vocabulary and Language Chunks

Write 10 sentences using vocabulary from the chapter.

1. _____
2. _____
3. _____
4. _____
5. _____
6. _____
7. _____
8. _____
9. _____
10. _____

My plan for practising is . . . _____

_____

_____

_____

CHAPTER 4
Food and Lifestyles

Thinking and Talking

Work with a partner to label the following statements about food as TRUE or FALSE. Discuss your answers with the class.

Statement	True	False
1. There is more sugar in lemons than in strawberries.		
2. The staple diet of more than 50 per cent of the world's population is rice.		
3. The remains of take-out food stores or "fast food" shops have been found in ancient Greek ruins.		
4. An average person eats about 35 tons of food during her or his lifetime.		
5. Ice cream originally comes from China. When Marco Polo returned to Italy from China in 1295, one of the things he brought back was a recipe for "ice milk", which was developed into ice cream.		
6. In France, people eat approximately 500,000,000 snails every year.		
7. In the past, salt was very rare and extremely valuable. People were often paid their wages in salt. The word "salary" comes from "salt."		
8. Frozen fruits and vegetables are sometimes more nutritious than fresh fruits and vegetables.		
9. If you are cold, you are more likely to feel hungry. Temperature affects our appetites.		
10. It takes about 3,500 calories to make a pound of fat.		
11. Peanuts are used in the making of dynamite.		
12. In the middle ages, people believed that the juice of a lemon could dissolve fish bones, and that is why fish is often served with a slice of lemon.		

Which of the above do you find the most difficult to believe? Explain why.

Communication Focus: Talking about Events in the Indefinite Past

We often give information about events in the past with no specific past time reference. We can use adverbs such as *ever, always, never, occasionally, often, several times,* and *recently*, to express this indefiniteness.

Examples	**Responses**
Have you ever eaten snake?	No I haven't, but I've had frogs' legs.
Has she ever drunk champagne?	No she hasn't, but she's drunk beer.
I have never had Indonesian food.	
We have always had cereal for breakfast.	
I have lost 20 lbs (9 kilos) recently!	

Grammar Note: Present Perfect Tense for Actions in the Indefinite Past

We use the present perfect tense to talk about an action in the past when there is no specific past time reference. To form the present perfect tense, use *have/has+ past participle*.

Examples

Have you had lunch yet?
Ellen has often eaten Chinese food.
My friends have never been to Italy.

 Please go to the website for more practice with this structure.

Speaking Activity 1

Walk around the classroom and talk to as many students as necessary until you find someone who has done the specific action. Make questions using "Have you ever . . . ?" When you find someone who fits the description in one of the boxes, write down his or her name. Then ask the person when and where they did that action. You may write a person's name only once.

SPEAKING STRATEGY

When you ask or answer questions, try to use complete sentences.

Find someone who	Question	Name	Where/When
. . . has had Italian food	Have you ever had Italian food?	Tina	She had Italian food at a restaurant last week.
. . . has eaten snake			
. . . has had rabbit			
. . . has drunk beer			
. . . has had ginseng tea			
. . . has eaten snails			
. . . has eaten eel			
. . . has tried champagne			
. . . has tried clams			

Find someone who	Question	Name	Where/When
. . . has consumed any kind of insect			
. . . has sipped espresso			
. . . has tried sushi and sashimi			
. . . has swallowed raw oysters			
. . . has tasted kimchi			
. . . has had chocolate covered strawberries			

Speaking Activity 2

Find out how many times people in your class have done the following activities. Each person will choose one of the questions and ask all the people in the class. Then make a poster about the food experiences of the people in your class.

Find out how many times people in the class . . .
have drunk champagne
have baked a birthday cake
have made a special dessert
have eaten raw oysters
have cooked lobster
have eaten fish they have caught
have looked up recipes on the internet
have gotten take-out food
have burned food while cooking
have drunk cappuccino
have gone to a vegetarian restaurant
have gone out to a restaurant recommended by a food critic
have made cocktails
have cooked soup from scratch
have bought food at a farmers' market
have baked a turkey
have shopped at an organic food market

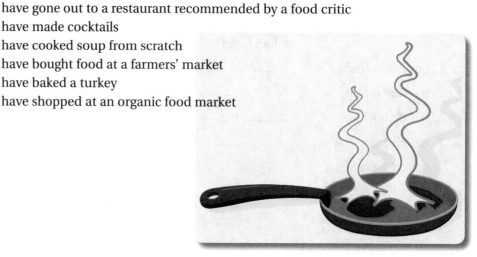

Speaking Activity 3

What are the most unusual foods in the world? Work with a partner. The following list describes some unusual foods from different countries. Choose the three foods that you think are the most unusual. Then choose the three foods that you would like to try and the three foods that you would never try. Compare your ideas to those of another group.

The Three Most Unusual Foods	Three Foods We Would Like to Try	Three Foods We Will Never Try
_____	_____	_____
_____	_____	_____
_____	_____	_____

Live octopus (South Korea)
Some people eat live octopus. The octopus is served alive and moving. People who like this dish recommend eating it quickly.

Grasshoppers (Uganda)
During the rainy season, you can buy grasshoppers at the local markets. They can be cooked or raw, and you can buy them with or without wings and legs.

Pigeon (France)
Pigeon is an expensive dish served in some of the best restaurants in France. It has a strong flavour and is popular in many parts of the world.

Durian (Malaysia)
This is a fruit with a very strong, stinky odour that some people have compared to the smell of rotting garbage. This spiky fruit may not be popular with foreigners but many Malaysians love it.

Grubs (Australia)
These white grubs are the larvae of moths and are very high in protein. They make a tasty snack. They were once an important food and a part of the diet of Aboriginal people living in the deserts of Australia.

Camel (Somalia, Saudi Arabia, and Egypt)
Camel can provide a large quantity of meat. The brisket, ribs, and loin are some of the better parts, but the hump is the best part. Camel meat tastes like beef.

Snake wine (Vietnam)
Some people say that snake wine has health benefits. It is an alcoholic drink made using snake blood with a snake (or sometimes another creature such as a scorpion) inside the bottle. It is best to drink this strong cocktail quickly.

Donkey (Italy)
In Italy, donkey meat is eaten much like Italian ham. People can easily get this meat in bars.

Buffalo/Bison (North America)
Buffalo meat is used in North America because it has only 10–12 per cent fat. It is a source of protein, niacin, vitamins B6 and B12, iron, phosphorus, potassium, and zinc, as well as other vitamins and minerals. People can use it in any recipe that calls for beef.

Ostrich (South Africa)
Ostrich is low in cholesterol and is considered healthier than other meats. It is popular all over the world. People eat everything from ostrich burgers to omelets made from ostrich eggs.

Fried tarantulas (Cambodia)
These huge, deadly spiders are sold at roadside stands and then fried with garlic. The legs are crispy but the stomach and internal organs are very gooey.

Communication Focus: Expressing Likes and Dislikes

Expressing Likes

Verbs	Examples
to like	John likes having seafood for dinner.
to love	His friends love to eat sushi.
to enjoy	Melissa really enjoys having lobster.
to feel like	Terry feels like going out to eat tonight.

Structures/Expressions	
to be fond of . . .	I am really fond of eating Chinese food. We are fond of diet drinks.
to be crazy about . . .	Sherry is crazy about chocolate. She wants to have it all the time.
. . . is my favourite	Yogurt is my favourite snack.

Expressing Dislikes

Verbs	Examples
(not) to care for	Joanna doesn't care for asparagus.
(not) to like	Abbas doesn't like turnips.
can't stand	Mary Ann can't stand eating raw fish.
to hate	My friend hates to eat leftovers.
to detest	Andrea detests spicy food.
to avoid	Mike avoids eating fried food.

Structures/Expressions	
. . . turn off	The smell of fish turns him off.
. . . to be put off	Janet is put off by smelly cheeses.

Grammar Note

The verbs *like, love, hate,* and *can't stand* can be followed by a gerund (base form of the verb + ing) or by an infinitive (to + base form of the verb).

Examples

I love eating out.
I love to eat out.

Other verbs such as *enjoy* and *avoid* can only be followed by a gerund or a noun. Expressions such as *to be fond of . . . , to be crazy about . . . ,* and *to care for . . .* end in prepositions, and these can only be followed by a noun or a gerund.

Example

Thelma enjoys having dessert. Her sister Anita doesn't care for sweets so she usually avoids eating dessert.

 Please go to the website for more practice with this structure.

Speaking Activity 4

Work in pairs. Interview your partner using the questions below. Report the
most interesting information to the class.

1. Do you live to eat or do you eat to live?

2. What is your favourite junk food? How often do you eat it?

3. What food or drink are you crazy about?

4. What food or drink do you avoid having? Explain.

5. What foods are you fond of? Please explain why.

6. What are some foods you don't care for?

7. What foods from your country do you miss having here?

8. What was your favourite food and drink when you were a child?

9. How does the food in your country compare to the food here? Which do
   you prefer to eat?

10. Is there anything you feel like having now?

SPEAKING STRATEGY

When you are answering
questions, check to see if
the listener understands by
asking questions such as
"Are you following me?" "Do
you know what I mean?" and
"Do you understand?"

Speaking Activity 5

Work in groups of four. Discuss these questions and record your answers. Make
a poster about the similarities and differences in your likes and dislikes.

Questions	Me	Partner #1	Partner #2	Partner #3
Describe the most memorable or delicious meal you have ever eaten. When and where did you eat it?				
What is the most wonderful drink you have ever had? When and where did you have it?				
What is the best dessert you have ever had? Where and when did you have it?				
What foods or drinks turn you off?				
What is the most unusual food or drink that you have ever had? Where and when did you have it?				

Listening 1

Before You Listen

Pre-listening Vocabulary

1. You will hear the following words and phrases in the discussion you are going to listen to on the audio CD. Work with a partner or by yourself to write the correct vocabulary next to the definitions.

Vocabulary

peculiar	irrational	texture	craving
compound	behaviour	biological	toxins
slimy	preference	interfere	override
nutrition	idiosyncrasy	nutrient	
heartburn	finicky	avoidance	

Definition	Vocabulary
food and drink which nourishes the body	_____
unusual, strange	_____
fussy about eating, not easily pleased	_____
the way a person acts and behaves	_____
act of staying away from, avoiding	_____
how the surface of something looks or feels	_____
a mixture or substance	_____
something that nourishes	_____
get in the way of	_____
poisons	_____
a favourite, a preferred thing	_____
take precedence over	_____
uncomfortable burning feeling in the lower part of the chest, indigestion	_____
a very strong desire	_____
slippery and greasy	_____
unconventional, unusual behaviour	_____
natural, from birth	_____
not reasonable	_____

2. You are going to listen to a discussion on the audio CD about why people have certain likes and dislikes in food. Write down two questions you have about this topic. Discuss your questions with a partner.

a) _____

b) _____

Listening for the Main Ideas

Listen to the interview once and answer the following questions.

1. What kind of show is this and why are the guests there?
2. What are some strange food behaviours that they discuss?
3. According to the discussion, why do people have likes and dislikes in food?
4. Did you find answers to your questions?

 Listening for Comprehension

Listen to the discussion on the audio CD again. As you listen, write out the definitions/explanations/examples the speakers give for the following words and phrases.

LISTENING STRATEGY

Listen for definitions or explanations to help you understand new or difficult words. Often definitions follow unusual or difficult words, to explain or clarify meaning. For example, in the phrase "your preferences, your likes and dislikes . . .", the word "preferences" is explained by what follows.

crazy about cucumbers   _____

a food aversion   _____

finicky or picky eaters   _____

food mixers   _____

idiosyncratic food behaviours   _____

nutrients   _____

crave   _____

supertasters   _____

originate   _____

the toddler years   _____

phobias   _____

bland   _____

Now, listen to the discussion again and answer the following questions.

1. What foods does Dr. Wu dislike?
2. What is one reason people don't eat red meat or other high protein foods?
3. Why do some people dislike green foods?
4. Why do we prefer to eat certain foods?
5. What are supertasters?
6. How do parents pass on their food likes and dislikes to their children?

Personalizing

With a partner, discuss some idiosyncratic food behaviours you each have and try to find an explanation for them.

Food Behaviour	Possible Explanation
_____	_____
_____	_____
_____	_____
_____	_____

Vocabulary and Language Chunks

Write the number of the expression next to the meaning. After checking your answers, choose six expressions and write your own sentences.

Expressions

1. the sight of
2. to break up with
3. to shy away from
4. high up on the list
5. to warn about
6. likely to
7. to pass on to someone
8. to pick out
9. to pass up
10. to open up to
11. no worries
12. to make up for
13. to do something about
14. on the other hand

Meanings

☐ no problem

☐ not to take an opportunity, to forgo

☐ close to the top of the list in importance

☐ probably will

☐ to leave behind, to give to somebody

☐ to choose

☐ to avoid

☐ to be ready to accept new things, to be receptive

☐ to give a warning or caution about

☐ from another point of view

☐ to take actions to fix or remedy

☐ to end a romantic relationship with

☐ to compensate for

☐ the appearance of

Listening 2

Before You Listen

In English, there are a great many idioms involving food that have nothing to do with the foods they mention. Can you think of any?

Try to guess the meanings of these idioms.

The apple of someone's eye
A hot potato
A couch potato
A piece of cake
To cry over spilt milk

Put the idioms into the sentences below.

1. John is not very active. He never goes to the gym or works out.
   He's a real _____.

2. The grandfather is crazy about his granddaughter. She is really

   _____.

3. None of the politicians wanted to talk about the nuclear energy plant. It's a
   real _____ in that community.

4. You can't do anything about the accident after it has already happened.
   There is no use in _____.

5. Learning to park the car was no problem for her. She says it was

   _____.

🎧 Listening for the Main Ideas

Listen to the show once and answer the following questions.

1. What kind of show is this?

2. Describe what the process is.

🎧 Listening for Comprehension

Listen to the show again. As you listen, write out the definitions of the following words and idioms.

Out to lunch   _____
Out of the frying pan and into the fire   _____
To take something with a grain of salt   _____
To salt away   _____
Wake up and smell the coffee   _____
Spill the beans   _____
(Have) egg on one's face   _____
Egg someone on   _____
In a nutshell   _____
A tough nut to crack   _____
To go nuts   _____

Personalizing

Work with two other people. Make a list of all the food idioms you can think of. Make up a dialogue using these idioms and/or the idioms from the listening task and perform your dialogue for the class. The class will ask you to explain those idioms they do not know.

Vocabulary and Language Chunks

Write the number of the expression next to the meaning. After checking your answers, choose six expressions and write your own sentences.

Expression	Meaning
1. at random	☐ reduce, decrease
2. to stump someone	☐ to have no more left/there is no more time left
3. to be good at something	☐ to overtake, become equal to someone
4. out of touch	☐ by chance
5. catch up to someone	☐ not quite right
6. put away	☐ insincere, false, double dealing
7. to be two-faced	☐ to make a mistake
8. to be out of (time)	☐ to be ahead, to be first
9. to be in the lead	☐ to confuse someone, to lead someone to make a mistake
10. slip up	☐ to be skilled at something
11. cut down	☐ not in contact with reality
12. a little bit off	☐ to save, not to use

Communication Focus: Stating Opinions

The following are some phrases you can use to express your opinions and ideas.

Structures/Expressions	Examples
(Personally) I feel/believe/think*	I personally feel that yoga is good for you.
From my point of view . . . In my opinion . . . In my view . . .	In my opinion, Chinese medicine can make you better.
As far as I am concerned . . . I'd say that . . ./I'd suggest that . . ./ I'd like to point out . . .	As far as I'm concerned, a positive attitude improves your health.
I suspect that . . .	I suspect that cooking destroys some of the nutrients in food.
I strongly believe/think/feel . . . I am certain/sure/positive that . . .	I strongly believe that a vegetarian diet is healthier.

Structures/Expressions	Examples
In my experience . . . To my mind . . . It seems to me . . . If you ask me . . .	In my experience, cooking a meal from scratch is healthier than eating out.
Not everybody will agree with me, but . . .	Not everybody will agree with me, but I believe that alternative medicine works better than conventional medicine.

Less Formal	Examples
If you ask me . . .	If you ask me, fast food is responsible for many illnesses.
You know what I think . . .	You know what I think, I think fast food is responsible for many illnesses.
Here's my two cents' worth.	Here's my two cents' worth. Exercise is the most important thing you can do for your health.
What I mean is . . . I'd like to say . . . I reckon . . .	I'd like to say that people who exercise are healthier.

* Using *I think* to express an opinion is very common in conversation.

Agreeing with Opinions

Diplomatic/Tactful/ Less Certain	Neutral	Very Certain/Positive
That's true. You have a point. OK/All right.	I believe you are right. I agree. That's how I feel, too. I think so, too.	Exactly! Of course! Absolutely! That's right! That goes without saying! Right on! I totally agree. I couldn't agree more.

Disagreeing with Opinions

Diplomatic/Tactful/ Less Certain	Neutral	Very Certain/Positive
I'm not sure I agree. I'm afraid I don't agree. I don't see it that way. I wouldn't say that.	I don't agree. I don't think that's right/true. I don't feel that way.	Absolutely not! I totally disagree. On the contrary . . . No way!

Supporting Opinions

There are a number of ways that you can support your opinions.

1. You can strengthen or support your opinion by giving reasons.

2. You can support your opinion by stating facts and experiences.

3. You can support your opinions by stating what experts or authorities say.

SPEAKING STRATEGY

Encourage yourself. You are just as good as others at getting your message across.

Speaking Activity 6

Work in groups of four. Do you agree or disagree with the following statements? State your opinions. Agree or disagree with the statements of the others in your group. Support your opinions and try to convince the others in the group, if they disagree with you.

Statement	Your Opinion (TRUE/FALSE)	Group Opinion
Laughter helps keep people healthy.		
People who have lots of friends (an active social life) are healthier.		
A positive attitude will improve your health.		
Diet is more important than exercise for losing weight.		
Drinking alcohol everyday is bad for your health.		
Vegetarians are usually healthier than non vegetarians.		
Vitamin supplements can give you energy and make you healthier.		
When you exercise, your fat turns to muscle.		
Eating four, five, or six times a day makes you put on weight.		
Drinking the right amount of water will help you burn calories.		
Love and marriage help people live longer.		

Speaking Activity 7

Work in pairs. Read these questions and express your opinions. Try to find support for your opinions. Then get together with another pair of students and talk about your agreements and disagreements.

1. Do you believe that there is a direct connection between the food we eat and the diseases we get? Please explain.

2. Do you think that people who take risks with their health (e.g., smokers, alcoholics, extreme sports enthusiasts, the obese, etc.) should be asked to pay more for health care or should not be eligible for health insurance?

3. Do you think smoking should be made illegal? Why or why not?

4. Which do you believe is the best—standard conventional medicine or alternative medical treatments, such as using herbs and acupuncture?

5. Do you believe that people have the right to choose to die?

6. Do you believe in mind over matter—that the mind has the power to cure illness?

7. Do you think that scientists will find a cure for major illnesses such as cancer, and that in the future people will live to be at least 150 years old?

8. Do you think scientists should continue to experiment with genetics in order to produce healthier, more intelligent, and more attractive human beings?

9. What part of the world is the best to live in from a health care point of view?

Listening 3

Before You Listen

Pre-listening Vocabulary

1. You will hear these words and phrases in the lecture. Work with a partner or by yourself to write the correct vocabulary next to the definitions.

Vocabulary

sip	conventional	stroke
outlook	obesity	organic food
to heal	genetic engineering	diabetes
consequences	well-being	blood pressure
ulcer	heart disease	to preserve
to rejuvenate	crops	arthritis
endangered	holistic	indigestion

Definitions	Vocabulary
drink slowly	_____
results, things that follow from an action or condition	_____
to keep safe, protect	_____
to make someone well	_____
in danger of dying out	_____
make young again, renew	_____
the rearranging of genes in living things	_____
the state of being very overweight, heaviness	_____
plants that are grown and gathered at harvest	_____
heart ailment, problem, illness	_____
food grown naturally without pesticides, herbicides, hormones, or any other additives	_____
a stoppage of blood flow to the brain	_____
the pressing of the blood against the walls of the arteries	_____
a medical disorder in which there is too much sugar (glucose) in the blood	_____
point of view, way of looking at the world	_____
inflammation of the joints with pain and stiffness	_____
a sore on the membrane lining the stomach or on another part of the digestive tract	_____
following usual or normal standards or customs	_____
sense of health and comfort	_____
dealing with the whole, the complete system	_____
problems with digestion, digestive disorders	_____

2. Work with a small group. Brainstorm all the things that you believe make people healthy and happy. Present your ideas to the class. Use opinion statements. Use statements of agreement and disagreement.

 Listening for the Main Ideas

Listen to the interview once. Circle the topics on the list below that are discussed in the lecture.

Diet and how food affects health

Mottos for health

Fast food and the consequences of eating it

The slow food movement

Italy

Farming

Vegetarian diets

Calorie-restricted diets

Benefits of exercise

Types of exercise

Effects of positive mental attitude

Intelligence

Alternative medicine

Types of alternative medicine

The mind-body connection

 Listening for Comprehension

Listen to the lecture again. As you listen, try to determine if the statements that the lecturer makes are facts or opinions. If the speaker uses an opinion expression, this is not a fact but only the speaker's opinion. If the speaker talks about research, this is a fact. Write FACT or OPINION after each statement.

1. Fast food consumption is why there is so much obesity, which leads to so many different diseases. _____

2. The slow food movement started in Italy in 1989 and grew into a social and political movement. _____

3. Fast food is responsible for large-scale farming practices, which destroy local foods and crops. _____

4. Vegetarians have reduced risks for heart disease, diabetes, and some forms of cancer. _____

5. Cooking destroys the nutrients in fruits and vegetables that our bodies need. _____

6. When animals are put on calorie-restricted diets they live much longer and do not fall ill with age-related diseases. _____

7. Water helps to remove the toxins or poisons from our systems, so the more you drink, the more poison you will get rid of. _____

8. As little as 20–30 minutes of exercise a day prevents early death. _____

9. There isn't anything as powerful as daily exercise for providing you with health, energy, and an improved outlook on life. _____

10. TCM is better than conventional medicine in curing illness. _____

Vocabulary and Language Chunks

Write the number of the expression next to the meaning. After checking your answers, choose six expressions and write your own sentences.

Expression	Meaning
1. simple and straightforward	☐ do away with, not to keep
2. no time like the present	☐ to investigate, to find out about
3. the earlier the better	☐ to be in an improved state/situation
4. better late than never	☐ as fast as lightning, extremely fast
5. home-cooked meal	☐ to have a role in something, to be responsible for a part of something
6. lightning speed	☐ in the event of, if a certain event should happen
7. you are what you eat	☐ plain and open, easy to understand
8. get rid of	☐ now is the best time
9. can-do attitude	☐ it's best to start early
10. play a part	☐ lunch or dinner which has been cooked by someone at home
11. in case of	☐ it's better to do something late than not to do it
12. to be better off	☐ enthusiasm and willingness to do something
13. look into	☐ the food we eat is responsible for the state of our health

Personalizing

Work with a partner. What are your opinions of the following? Do you agree with the lecturer? Do you agree with each other? Try to support your opinions.

Topic	My Opinion	My Partner's Opinion
fast food		
the slow food movement		
positive thinking		
alternative medicine		
meditation and yoga		
exercise		
vegetarians		
calorie restricted diets		
genetic engineering		
organic food		

Speaking Activity 8

Work with a partner. Interview each other. Discuss these questions and report the two most interesting facts to the class.

1. Are you afraid of going to the doctor or the dentist? What is the reason for your fear?

2. Have you ever been in the hospital? How long did you stay? How did you feel about it?

3. What disease are you most afraid of?

4. Do you take garlic, ginseng, Echinacea, or other herbs or medicines to cure or prevent illness? Why or why not?

5. Why do you think women live longer than men?

6. Why do so many more people get cancer and Alzheimer's disease than ever before? What can be done to prevent this?

7. According to the World Health Organization, about 3,000 people commit suicide every day. Why are so many people committing suicide?

8. What is the most important health problem or health issue today?

9. Do you trust doctors completely? Why or why not?

10. Would you prefer to go to a male or female doctor? Explain.

11. What do you think of the cosmetic surgery available today? Would you like to have cosmetic surgery?

12. People live longer today than they did 100 years ago. Do you think they are happier than they were then?

Speaking Activity 9

Divide the class into two groups. Choose a topic to debate. Each group will select either the FOR or the AGAINST statements. Make the arguments listed, support them, and add to them.

Each time one side presents an argument, the other side has the opportunity to respond to the argument until the teams have no more arguments to make. The entire class will vote on which team won the debate.

Debate topics

1. People are better off today than they were 100 years ago.

   FOR Statements

   a)   People today live longer.

   b)   People today have more health care, more doctors, and more hospitals.

   c)   We know more about disease and the body.

   d)   We have better and more kinds of medicines.

   e)   Science has made our lives easier. For example, we have jet planes, big screen TVs, computers, and all kinds of appliances.

   f)   Transportation is better today, including cars, subways, and buses.

   g)   Communications are much better, including cellphones and the Internet.

   h)   People have more entertainment options available today, including movies, sports, and plays.

AGAINST Statements

a) People may live longer, but they don't feel they have a purpose in life. Fewer people are religious or have goals.

b) There seems to be more disease than before; for example, there are more cases of cancer, Alzheimer's, allergies, etc.

c) There are many diseases for which there are no cures. New viruses and other diseases have appeared in the past 100 years.

d) Many people in the world cannot afford the fancy new medications.

e) Many people cannot afford the latest gadgets. The latest gadgets also quickly break down and need to be replaced, which creates more garbage.

f) Cars and buses are contributing to the pollution of the world.

g) Better communication has made it easier for people to be cheated by criminals.

h) Much entertainment is violent and geared to the lowest common denominator—the bored and under-educated.

2. Nature and the natural world are better and healthier for us than what modern society has created.

FOR Statements

a) Many of the foods we eat are filled with artificial colours and flavours, which lead to illnesses.

b) When we change nature, for example, by building dams like the Three Gorges Dam in China or by cutting down rainforests, we are destroying plants and animals, and we don't know what the results of this will be in the future.

c) Our bodies were designed to live in a certain way. The increase in noise, our sedentary lifestyle, and the pollution in the cities leads to more stress and physical and mental illness.

d) We are producing garbage at increased rates and we are polluting nature by dumping this garbage into the oceans or into landfill sites.

e) We have created enough weapons of mass destruction to destroy the world and this leads to stress, worry, and fighting with other countries.

AGAINST Statements

a) We need to increase the amount of food we produce because of the increase in the world's population. Therefore, sometimes we need to use colour and artificial flavours.

b) When we build new dams or cut down forests or build roads, we are doing this to improve people's lives—to make travel easier and to make communication better.

c) People have always had stress. Thousands of years ago, when hunters failed to find food, they were stressed too. There are more people in the world, so naturally there has to be more noise and more pollution. Stress can be a good thing. It motivates us to work harder.

d) Because there are so many more people, there will be more garbage. Where else can we put the garbage if not in the oceans and in the ground?

e) We need the weapons we have to protect our society and our country from others who may want to destroy it.

Pronunciation

Rhythm: The stressed and unstressed words in English sentences.

Rule 1: In normal fast speech, English speakers stress the following words:

Nouns	Verbs	Adjectives	Adverbs
food	grow	good	very
class	get	nice	fast
book	buy	cheap	hard

Negatives	WH Question Words	Demonstratives	
don't	where	this	these
can't	how	that	those

These are called content words because they carry the meaning of the sentence.

Rule 2: Do not stress the other words such as those in the following list. These are the words which tell us about the grammatical relations in the sentence.

Personal Pronouns and Possessive Adjectives		Articles	Short Prepositions
he	his	a	for
she	her	the	to
him			of
them	their		

Conjunctions	Auxiliary Verbs	Relative Pronouns
and	did/do	who/whom
or	have/has	which
but	can/will	that
because		
when		
if		

 Pronunciation Activity 1

Listen and underline the stressed words in these sentences.

1. Birds look for worms.
2. The birds are looking for the worms.
3. Don't eat apples.
4. We don't eat the apples.
5. Buy books.
6. I'll buy the books.
7. Learn new words.
8. I'm learning the new words.
9. George does special exercises.
10. George has been doing the special exercises.

Each pair of sentences has the same number of stressed syllables and it should take about the same time to say both sentences regardless of the number of words there are in them. In English, speakers give equal time to the number of stresses, not syllables in a sentence. English is a stress-timed language. Practise saying the sentences with a partner.

Pronunciation Activity 2

Limericks are rhyming poems that are often written for children. They are fun to use to practise stressed and unstressed words. Read the following limerick and discuss any new words. Now listen to the limerick and underline the stressed words.

> There was a young lady whose chin,
> Resembled the point of a pin.
> So she had it made sharp,
> And purchased a harp,
> And played many tunes with her chin.

Practise saying the limerick with your partner.

Check your answers against the Answer Key to correctly identify the stressed words.

Listen to this limerick, and underline the stressed words.

> There was an old man with a beard,
> Who said, "It is just as I feared!—
> Two owls and a hen,
> Four larks and a wren,
> Have all built their nests in my beard!"

Check your answers against the Answer Key to correctly identify the stressed words.

Practise saying this limerick with a partner. Then try to write one with your partner.

 Pronunciation Activity 3

Listen to the speaker and repeat the sentences. Then work with a partner. Listen to your partner say the sentences. Did your partner stress the right words? Now change places.

1. I'm sorry you're sick.
2. Can I talk to you now?
3. Thank you for helping.
4. She can do it alone.
5. Where did he go?
6. What can I do?
7. I'd like her to help us move.
8. What's the number of the store?
9. Where did you leave the package?
10. How long do I have to finish the test?
11. Can I get you coffee or tea?
12. We are going to walk to the store.

Pronunciation Activity 4

Listen to the material on the audio CD and write the word that is missing in the following sentences. Practise saying these sentences with a partner.

1. She's going _____ the door.

2. It's really up _____ them.

3. What's _____ supper?

4. I'll have _____ see.

5. It's three hundred _____ thirty.

6. It's either thirteen _____ thirty.

7. Can you go ____ see who's at the door?

8. They're brother _____ sister.

9. They're three _____ a quarter.

10. Do you have a lot _____ do?

11. This party is _____ husbands _____ wives.

12. Please wait _____ us.

There are many words in English which are joined by *and*. Listen to the audio CD and fill in the missing words. These are some food-related expressions. Repeat the expressions after the speaker.

cream _____ _____   cheese _____ _____
sweet _____ _____   bacon _____ _____
knives _____ _____   meat _____ _____
ham _____ _____   salt _____ _____
cups _____ _____   milk _____ _____
peanut butter _____ _____   surf _____ _____
bread _____ _____   fish _____ _____

These are some additional expressions joined by *and*. Listen to the speaker on the audio CD and fill in the missing words. Repeat them after the speaker.

war _____ _____   aches _____ _____
back _____ _____   rights _____ _____
men _____ _____   trial _____ _____
husbands _____ _____   pros _____ _____
brothers _____ _____   neat _____ _____
uncles _____ _____   sick _____ _____

Work with a partner. Practise saying the expressions to each other. Remember to reduce *and*. Make up a dialogue using as many of these expressions as you can.

Pronunciation Activity 5

Listen to the speaker on the audio CD and write out the pronunciation of the function words on the chart.

Function Words	Pronunciation in Normal Fast Speech	Examples
Prepositions		
of	_____	a loaf of bread
	_____	a bunch of flowers
for	_____	a gift for you
to	_____	go to work
at	_____	at school
Conjunctions		
and	_____	cat and mouse game
or	_____	love it or leave it
Pronouns		
him	_____	Did you ask him?
her	_____	Did you tell her?
them	_____	Did you introduce them?
you	_____	Do you like it?
Articles		
a	_____	a cup of coffee
an	_____	an elephant
the	_____	on the floor
Auxiliary verbs		
do/does/did	_____	Where do you live?
	_____	What did he do?
	_____	What kind does she like?
have/has/had	_____	She should have stayed.
	_____	He has worked.
	_____	We had finished.
can	_____	Can you do it?

Listen to the speaker on the audio CD and write out the phrases you hear. Check your answers with a partner and then with the teacher. Then, make up a dialogue using as many of the phrases as you can.

1. _____
2. _____
3. _____
4. _____
5. _____
6. _____
7. _____
8. _____
9. _____
10. _____
11. _____

Pronunciation Activity 6

Listen to these sentences. Write the words that you hear in the blank spaces provided. Example: Why <u>did she</u> start crying? When you have finished, practise saying the sentences with a partner.

1. He's never practised _____ singing.

2. When _____ it be ready?

3. When _____ moving _____ country?

4. Have _____ introduced _____ each other?

5. Has _____ mother told _____ story?

6. That's what _____ did.

7. I told _____ get ready.

8. We showed _____ store.

9. _____ had a bad experience.

10. _____ know _____?

11. _____ I try _____ help _____?

12. _____ do _____ a favour?

Pronunciation Activity 7

In normal fast speech, English speakers usually join the regular verb ending –ed to the following pronoun. Repeat these sentences after the speaker. Then practise saying them with a partner.

1. We told him the answers.

2. She picked them up.

3. We helped her do her homework.

4. She sends them cards at Christmas.

5. Her father helps her do the shopping.

6. She kicked him out.

7. The music relaxed her and she fell asleep.

8. The game tired them out.

9. I baked her a cake for her birthday.

10. He phoned her up.

Pronunciation Activity 8

The phrases in the following table relate to the do's and don'ts of losing weight. Work with a partner to match up the phrases in the two columns. When you have finished, read the do's and don'ts to each other. Discuss them and tell the class which two you think are the best.

Do enjoy . . .	at least nine glasses of water daily.
Do include . . .	all the fat from your meat.
Do have . . .	foods which are fried with butter and oil.
Do trim . . .	say no to sugar in coffee, tea, or pop.
Don't eat . . .	if you do, the weight loss will come from losing water and muscle.
Don't drink your calories—	without a plan.
Don't starve yourself—	exercise in your lifetime plan.
Don't go to a restaurant . . .	a variety of foods from the different food groups.

Communicating in the Real World

Try to use your English to talk to people outside your class. Work with a partner to make up a questionnaire asking four to eight questions about one of the following topics. Then find several people who are not in your class and ask the questions. Report what you learned to the class.

Topics: fast food, genetically-modified foods, alternative medicine, exercise, happiness, and the health care system.

Self Evaluation

Rate yourself (using a scale of 0–5, where "5" is the highest ranking) and write your comments in each section of the chart. Show the chart to your teacher and discuss your strengths and weaknesses.

Topic	Good (5, 4)	Improving (3, 2)	Needs more work (1, 0)
Grammar and Language Functions 1. Talking about events in the indefinite past 2. Expressing likes and dislikes 3. Food idioms 4. Stating opinions; agreeing/disagreeing; supporting opinions			
Speaking Strategies 1. When you ask or answer questions, try to use complete sentences. 2. When you are answering questions, check to see if the listener understands by asking questions such as "Are you following me?" "Do you know what I mean?" and "Do you understand?" 3. Encourage yourself. You are just as good as others at getting your message across. 4. What other speaking strategies did you use?			
Listening Strategies 1. Listen for definitions or explanations to help you understand new or difficult words. Example: ". . . your *preferences*, your likes and dislikes . . ." The word *preferences* is defined by what follows. 2. As you listen, formulate questions about points that are not clear to you. This will help to clarify the meaning when you discuss these points later. 3. What other listening strategies did you use?			
Pronunciation Stressed and unstressed words			

Vocabulary and Language Chunks

Write 10 sentences using vocabulary from the chapter.

1. _____
2. _____
3. _____
4. _____
5. _____
6. _____
7. _____
8. _____
9. _____
10. _____

My plan for practising is . . . _____

_____

_____

CHAPTER 5
Leisure, Sports, and Entertainment

Thinking and Talking

In our LEISURE we reveal what kind of people we are.
> —Ovid, Roman poet

Cultivated LEISURE is the aim of man.
> —Oscar Wilde, British writer

As a group discuss what these quotations mean. What's your own idea of leisure?

SPEAKING STRATEGY

When you want to say something, use body language and eye contact to let people know you are ready to speak. You can look at the speaker to let her or him know that you are waiting to speak. You can also lean forward or lean towards the speaker.

Speaking Activity 1

Work with a group. In a 2008 poll about favourite leisure activities in the United States, the activities listed in the table below were mentioned. Work with your group to rank the top seven activities that you think Americans chose. Give "1" to the most popular activity, "2" to the second most popular, and so on. Present your ranking to the class.

- [ ] travelling
- [ ] playing music
- [ ] shopping
- [ ] going to the movies
- [ ] gardening
- [ ] eating out
- [ ] dancing

- [ ] watching TV
- [ ] reading
- [ ] doing exercise such as weight lifting
- [ ] fishing
- [ ] computer activities
- [ ] spending time with family and friends

- [ ] spending time with pets/animals
- [ ] renting movies
- [ ] playing team sports
- [ ] golf
- [ ] walking
- [ ] hunting

Communication Focus: Stating and Asking about Preferences

Structures/Expressions	Examples
. . . would rather . . .	He would rather watch TV than go for a walk. Would you rather listen to pop or classical music?
. . . prefer . . .	She prefers dancing to swimming. Do you prefer Indian or Thai food?
I like . . . better than . . .	I like playing baseball better than playing hockey. Which do you like better, going out to a movie or renting a video?
I don't like . . . as much as . . .	I don't like playing hockey as much as playing baseball.

103

Speaking Activity 2

Tell your partner about two preferences in the following categories. Find out about your partner's preferences.

Categories	Your Preferences	Your Partner's Preferences
Which active leisure activities do you prefer?		
yoga		
kickboxing		
playing soccer		
playing ping pong		
Other:		
Which passive leisure activities do you prefer?		
watching movies		
reading		
gambling		
playing music		
computer activities		
Other:		
Which outdoor activities do you prefer?		
hiking		
swimming		
walking		
gardening		
fishing		
Other:		
Which social activities do you prefer?		
entertaining		
dancing		
singing in a choir		
spending time with family and friends		
socializing with neighbours and acquaintances		
Other:		

Speaking Activity 3

Work in groups of four. Find out the similarities and differences between you and your classmates. Discuss why you prefer these activities to others.

Name	What is Your Favourite Sport?	What is Your Favourite Leisure Activity?	What Sport or Activity Do You Dream of Taking Up?
_____	_____	_____	_____
_____	_____	_____	_____
_____	_____	_____	_____
_____	_____	_____	_____

Speaking Activity 4

Work in groups of four. Rank these activities in the order that they appeal to your group. Everyone must agree. Choose someone from the group to report to the class about the top five activities you chose, why you chose them, and any special equipment you would need to do these activities.

Activity/Sport	Ranking	Special Equipment
Using the computer	_____	_____
Mountain climbing	_____	_____
Sailing	_____	_____
Bicycle riding	_____	_____
Drawing/painting	_____	_____
Playing an instrument	_____	_____
Photography	_____	_____
Coin/stamp collecting	_____	_____
Baseball	_____	_____
Soccer	_____	_____
Formula 1 racing	_____	_____
Hockey	_____	_____
Gliding	_____	_____
Windsurfing	_____	_____
Fishing	_____	_____

Listening 1

Before You Listen

Pre-listening Vocabulary

1. You will hear these words and phrases in the interview you are going to listen to. Work with a partner or by yourself to write the correct vocabulary next to the definitions.

Vocabulary

extreme	risk	individual	overwhelming	diving
enthusiast	focus	thrills	cliff	board
folks	image	element	eliminate	challenge
artificial	freestyle	reveal	gear	hype
track	alternative	parachuting	surfing	

Definition	Vocabulary
steep rock face	_____
a piece of wood	_____
jumping from an airplane using a light material canopy	_____
feelings of great excitement	_____
people who are enthusiastic about a hobby	_____
the point attention is paid to	_____
person, human being	_____
component	_____
another option or possibility	_____
synthetic, created by man	_____
severe, excessive, intense, great	_____
contest, test	_____
riding waves in the ocean using a board	_____
remove, do away with	_____
overpowering, great, huge	_____
jumping into water or through air	_____
equipment	_____
people	_____
pathway, trail	_____
show	_____
picture	_____
free to choose any style or way	_____
danger, hazard	_____
publicity, advertising	_____

2. Work with a partner. You are going to listen to an interview with a sports journalist about extreme sports. Discuss and list extreme sports that you know about. Then talk about what you want to find out about extreme sports.

Extreme Sports We Know About	What We Want to Learn about Extreme Sports

 LISTENING STRATEGY

It's not necessary to understand every word when you are listening. Focus on the overall message when you hear something for the first time.

 Listening for the Main Ideas

Listen to the interview once and answer these questions.

1. What is the purpose of this show?

2. Who are the people on the show and what are they discussing?

3. What are some differences between extreme sports and traditional sports?

4. How does the host of the radio show feel about extreme sports?

Listening Comprehension

Listen to the interview again. As you listen, write down two points that you hear about the following topics.

Extreme sports

1. _____

2. _____

The focus in extreme sports

1. _____

2. _____

Who do extreme sports appeal to?

1. _____

2. _____

BMX

1. _____

2. _____

Skateboarding

1. _____

2. _____

BASE jumping

1. _____

2. _____

Paintball

1. _____

2. _____

Zorbing

1. _____

2. _____

Volcano boarding

1. _____

2. _____

Why do people do these new sports?

1. _____

2. _____

LISTENING STRATEGY

Identify and make a list of words that you do not understand and then find out their meanings.

Personalizing

Work in groups of four. Decide as a group which two extreme sports you would like to try and which ones you would never try. Present your selections to the class and explain why you have selected each sport.

Vocabulary and Language Chunks

Write the number of the expression next to the meaning. After checking your answers, choose six expressions and write your own sentences.

Expressions

1. to keep someone up to date
2. to come out in droves
3. to get the point
4. in contrast
5. to take your breath away
6. to come to mind
7. to sweep the world
8. to hold someone back
9. to take part in
10. fair play

Meanings

☐ proper, correct conduct

☐ to participate

☐ to stop someone

☐ to spread through the world

☐ on the other hand, conversely

☐ to provide the latest information to someone

☐ to attend in huge numbers

☐ to understand the main idea

☐ to cause someone to be out of breath due to shock or hard exercise

☐ to appear in thoughts, in the mind

SPEAKING STRATEGY

When you are ready to speak, let the others know by making polite sounds such as *ah*, *um*, *OK*, or *I think* . . . to signal that you are ready to speak.

Speaking Activity 5

Work in groups of four. Together choose five sports for each category. List them in order (for example, give "1" to the most dangerous activity, "2" to the second most dangerous, and so on). When you have completed the charts, think of your own categories for these sports. The group which comes up with the most categories is the winner.

The Most Dangerous	The Most Exciting	The Most Fun	The Most Relaxing
_____	_____	_____	_____
_____	_____	_____	_____
_____	_____	_____	_____
_____	_____	_____	_____
_____	_____	_____	_____

tobogganing	boxing	skydiving
wrestling	volcano boarding	cycling
hockey	canoeing	football
karate	golf	skateboarding
water skiing	skiing	basketball
baseball	auto racing	soccer
swimming	fishing	zorbing
ping pong	yoga	volleyball
paint ballx	BASE jumping	windsurfing
bowling	billiards	scuba diving
jogging	weightlifting	

Communication Focus: Expressing Ability and Inability

Use *can*, *could*, or *to be able to* to express ability.

Affirmative	Negative	Interrogative
Present		
I can swim very well.	He can't run.	Can you windsurf?
I am able to swim very well.	He isn't able to run.	Are you able to windsurf?
Past		
I could swim very well.	He couldn't run.	Could you windsurf?
I was able to swim very well.	He wasn't able to run.	Were you able to windsurf?
Future		
I will be able to swim.	He won't be able to run.	Will you be able to windsurf?

Grammar Note

Can/could and *to be able to* both express ability. The meanings are the same, except in the past tense. In the past, *could* means past ability only. *Was/were able to* also mean past ability, but it can also express past ability and accomplishment.

Examples

She was able to win the gold medal at the Olympics because she could skate very well.

As a child, my brother could run very fast. He was able to win the marathon.

 Please go to the website for more practice with this structure.

Speaking Activity 6

Work with a partner. On your own, make a list of all the activities and sports that you were able to do five to ten years ago, those you can do at the present time, and those you would like to do in the future. Compare lists with your partner and discuss the similarities and differences.

Five to Ten Years Ago	Present Time	In the Future
_____	_____	_____
_____	_____	_____
_____	_____	_____
_____	_____	_____
_____	_____	_____

Communication Focus: Expressing Advisability

We often use *should* to express advisability.

Affirmative	Negative	Interrogative
Present		
You should exercise more.	He shouldn't eat a heavy meal before swimming.	Should I join a health club?

Other Expressions/Structures to Express Advisability	Examples
It's a good idea . . .	It's a good idea to wear a helmet if you are cycling.
It's advisable . . .	It's advisable to wear knee pads when you are learning to skateboard.
. . . had better . . .*	You had better learn the vocabulary or else you will fail.
. . . ought to . . .**	You ought to stretch before running.

*. . . *had better* is very strong. We often use it to warn people.
** *Ought to* is not often used in negatives or questions.

Should is a very strong way to express advisability. We don't use *should* when speaking to peers or people of higher status. Instead, a coach might use this with a trainee, a teacher speaking to a student, or a doctor speaking to a patient.

 Please go to the website for more practice with this structure.

Speaking Activity 7

Work in groups of three. Ask each other the following questions and write down the responses. When you have finished, join another group and discuss the similarities and differences amongst you.

Questions	Partner #1	Partner #2
1. What bad habits do you have? What should you do about them?		
2. What should you do more often?		
3. Is there anyone you should see more often?		
4. What should you do to make your family happier?		
5. What should you do to make yourself a better person?		
6. What should you do to make yourself healthier?		
7. What should the government do to make our lives better?		
8. In what ways should society change?		
9. What do you think is the most serious problem at this time? What should we do about it?		
10. What should the teacher do to make learning easier and better?		
11. What should your classmates do to improve the learning conditions?		
12. Name a famous person. What do you think he or she should do?		
13. What are some things you think you had better do to make your life easier or better?		

Speaking Activity 8

Work in groups of three. Rank these problems in the order of their importance to your group. For example, "1" is the most important problem, "2" is the second most important, and so on. Then decide what you think people should do about the problem.

☐ Cost of living	_____
☐ Crime	_____
☐ Public transportation	_____
☐ Quality of medical care	_____
☐ Traffic	_____
☐ Quality of education	_____
☐ Discrimination against women or minorities	_____

Communication Focus: Expressing Advisability/ Inadvisability and Reprimanding

The past form of *should* requires the auxiliary verb *have + the past participle*.

Affirmative	**Negative**	**Interrogative**
Janice should have apologized for being late. (But she didn't.)	Allan shouldn't have lied. (But he did.)	Should we have invited the whole class to the party? (But we didn't.)

Please note that there is a change of meaning in the past form.

Examples

They should have played volleyball. (This means they *didn't play* volleyball.)

Anita shouldn't have gone running. (This means Anita *went* running.)

We use the past form of *should* to express different communicative functions, such as expressing regret, criticism, and reprimands.

Expressing Regret

Examples

I shouldn't have spent all my money on clothes.

I should have started studying for the test earlier.

Criticizing

Examples

The students shouldn't have cheated. It was wrong.

The class should have started on time.

Reprimanding

Examples

You shouldn't have driven so fast.

You should have been polite to the police officer.

 Please go to the website for more practice with this structure.

Speaking Activity 9

Work with a partner. Ask each other about some regrets you have about the past. Ask and answer the following questions. Use *should/shouldn't have + past participle.*

1. What regrets do you have about your education?
2. What regrets do you have about your personal life?
3. What regrets do you have about your family?
4. What do you regret about something you did recently?
5. What do you regret about something you didn't do?

Listening 2

Before You Listen

Pre-listening Vocabulary

1. You will hear these words and phrases in the lecture. Work with a partner or by yourself to write the correct vocabulary next to the definitions.

Vocabulary

violence	crime	sadistic	justifiable
bystander	concern	current	to torture
entertainment	to glorify	majority	evidence
obvious	graphic	fantasy	exposure
to fascinate	lyrics	to murder	desensitize

Definition	Vocabulary
leisure activities which give us pleasure	_____
to put to death, kill	_____
aggressive, hostile, violent actions	_____
offence which is against the law	_____
to praise highly, exalt	_____
words to songs	_____
to interest, to attract, to enthrall	_____
proof	_____
violent, hostile, belligerent	_____
act of showing, disclosing, exposing	_____
worry	_____
to make someone less sensitive	_____
of the present time	_____
to make someone suffer, to make someone feel pain	_____
realistic, vivid	_____
understandable, able to give a reason for	_____
clear, plain, easy to see	_____
on-looker, a person who watches something, witness	_____
daydream, desire, fancy	_____
the greater part, greater number, more than 50 per cent	_____

2. Work with a partner to discuss the following questions.

   a) Describe a movie or TV show with violence in it that you saw recently.

   b) What was the reason for the violence? In your opinion, was the violence necessary?

   c) Imagine that you are a parent. How much violence would you like your children to see? What are your reasons?

Listening for the Main Ideas

Listen to the lecture on the audio CD once and then answer these questions.

1. What kinds of entertainment is the lecture about?

2. What main points does the speaker make about violence in entertainment?

3. What does the research say about violence in entertainment?

4. What are the lecturer's feelings and opinions of violence in the media?

Listening Comprehension

Listen to the lecture again. This time, you are going to take notes. One way to take notes is to write down information that you hear about a topic or main idea. The main topics in the lecture have been written down for you. Write notes about the details under each topic.

The details for the first three topics have already been done for you as an example. Listen to the lecture to see how the notes for the first three topics summarize the points the lecturer makes. Use these examples to help you take notes.

You may listen to the lecture more than once if necessary.

Example

Violence in entertainment
in TV
movies
music
video games
Internet

Increase in TV violence
proof—7 yr. study, violence
increased—378%
2001—40 acts of violence/hr
today—much higher

Violence in the past
Egyptians—play—god—killings
humans—always—interested—violence
always—role—violence—entertainment

Statistics in the USA

_____

_____

_____

Research

_____

_____

_____

American Movies and TV

_____

_____

_____

Music and Music Videos

_____

_____

_____

Video Games

_____

_____

_____

Internet Websites

_____

_____

_____

Experts' Opinions

_____

_____

_____

Lecturer's Opinion

_____

_____

_____

 LISTENING STRATEGY

If you can connect the information that you hear in a listening to your own knowledge, experiences, and opinions, you will have a deeper understanding of the information and will be able to evaluate it better.

Personalizing

Work with a group. As a group, what is your opinion about the following topics? What are your reasons? Decide if there should be some control of what we see in entertainment and who should control it.

Topic	My Opinion	Group Opinion and Support
Violence in TV shows		
Violence in movies		
Violence in music and music videos		
Violence in video games		
Violence on the Internet		

Vocabulary and Language Chunks

Write the number of the expression next to the meaning. After checking your answers, choose six expressions and write your own sentences.

Expressions

1. to put on a play
2. copycat
3. play a role
4. to be a cause of
5. slow-motion
6. the vast majority
7. to move into the mainstream
8. the current trend
9. to be all over
10. tend to

Meanings

☐ have a tendency to

☐ to perform a play

☐ to be responsible for

☐ to be everywhere

☐ imitation, something that is copied

☐ to have a part in

☐ the latest fashion

☐ moving more slowly than in real life

☐ to become very commonplace

☐ much greater number than 50 per cent

Communication Focus: Summarizing

We summarize when we relate the highlights or main points of longer written or spoken texts such as articles, stories, or reports.

Structures/Expressions	Examples
The main points are . . .	The main points are that there has been an increase in violence in the media and that this has a negative effect on society.
The most important issues are . . .	The most important issues are what children watch on TV, and how many hours they watch.
In summary, . . .	In summary, the writer believes that society suffers from the focus on violence that we see in entertainment.
To conclude, . . .	To conclude, she feels parents, teachers, doctors, and all of society should protect children from the impact of violence in the media.
To make a long story short, . . .	To make a long story short, she can't stand all the violence we are exposed to every day.
In a nut shell, . . .	In a nut shell, she believes we need to do something to prevent media violence from causing harm to children and to society.
To sum it all up, . . .	To sum it all up, she would like to see more controls on media violence, on children's TV viewing habits, and on society's exposure to violence.

Speaking Activity 10

Work with a partner. Discuss your feelings and ideas about the following topics. Then summarize your discussions for the class.

Topics	Main Points
Violence in society in general	_____
Warfare	_____
Terrorism	_____
Censorship	_____
Children's rights	_____
Freedom of speech	_____
Individual rights	_____
Women's rights	_____

Communication Focus: Expressing Possibility/Speculating

When we want to say there is a 50 per cent chance of something being true in the present or in the future, we use these structures and expressions.

Affirmative	Negative	Interrogative
The pictures **might frighten** the child.	The pictures **might not frighten** the child.	**Might** the pictures **frighten** the child?*
The story **could upset** her.		**Could** the story **upset** her?
The program **may scare** them.	The program **may not scare** them.	

*This structure is formal sounding and is not is not often used.

Expressions

It's possible . . .   It's possible that the pictures will frighten the child.

Perhaps . . .   Perhaps the story will upset her.

Maybe . . .   Maybe the program will scare them.

 Please go to the website for more practice with this structure.

Speaking Activity 11

Work with a partner. What changes do you think might take place in the next 20 years? What could happen in the following areas? When you have finished, join another pair of students. Compare your ideas. What similarities and differences did you find? Summarize your discussions for the class.

Topics	What Changes Do You Think We Might See in 20 Years?
TV	
music	
video games	
Internet	
websites	
movies	
cars	
planes	
education	
children	
men	
women	
society	

Speaking Activity 12

Work with a partner. Talk about where you each might be and what you might be doing ten years from now. Once you have finished, speculate about three of your classmates. Show them your ideas. Find out if anyone had any ideas about you. Report similarities to the class.

Name	Place	Activities
_____	_____	_____
_____	_____	_____
_____	_____	_____
_____	_____	_____
_____	_____	_____

Communication Focus: Expressing Possibility in the Past/ Speculating about Past Events

When we want to say that there is a 50 per cent chance of something being true in the past, we use the structures and expressions outlined below.

Affirmative	Negative	Interrogative
They might have gone to the party.	They might not have gone to the party.	Might they have gone to the party?*
They could have returned to the hotel.		Could they have returned to the hotel?
They may have learned to play bridge.	They may not have learned to play bridge.	

* This structure is formal sounding and is not often used.

Expressions

Possibly . . .	They have gotten lost, possibly.
Maybe . . .	Maybe they have gotten lost.
Perhaps . . .	Perhaps they have gotten lost.

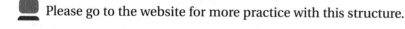 Please go to the website for more practice with this structure.

Speaking Activity 13

Work with a partner to speculate about what might have happened in the following mysterious situations. When you have finished, join another pair of students and share your answers.

Topic	What Might Have Happened? What Could Have Happened? What May Have Happened?
Why did the dinosaurs disappear?	_____
Did Atlantis exist? What happened to it?	_____
How did the ancient Egyptians build gigantic structures like the pyramids?	_____
Who invented writing?	_____
Why did the Neanderthals disappear?	_____
How did man discover fire?	_____
How did human language start?	_____
What happened to the Mayan civilization?	_____
Who built Stonehenge?	_____
Who put up all the statues on Easter Island?	_____
Your mystery:	_____

Pronunciation: Linking Words in Connected Speech

In normal fast speech in English, words can be joined over word boundaries. If speakers don't do this, they may sound abrupt, the rhythm of the phrase may be distorted, or, at worst, the phrase may be unintelligible to the listener. We link words under several different conditions.

Condition 1

In English, when a word begins with a vowel and is preceded by a word ending in a consonant, the sound of the consonant is linked to the following vowel. For example, "Pick it up," "Turn it on," and "Hand one over."

 Pronunciation Activity 1

1. Listen to the material on the audio CD and underline the places where the links occur. Then repeat the sentences after the speaker.

a) I got up at eleven.
b) I love it.
c) All washed up.
d) Watch it.
e) March on.
f) Watch out.

g) We are doing it over.
h) Give up.
i) Step over it.
j) Breathe out.
k) Hand out the papers.

l) It's up on the shelf.
m) We found him.
n) That's a lot of oranges.
o) This afternoon at five o'clock.

2. Work with a partner. Say the sentences to each other. Make sure that you are each linking the words together.

3. Choose six sentences from this list and make up a dialogue which you will do for the class.

Condition 2

When a word ends with the consonants *p, b, t, d, k, g,* and the next word begins with a consonant, the final consonants are pronounced but not released, that is they are not strongly pronounced. This means that we hold the final consonant until we are ready to say the next word.

 Pronunciation Activity 2

1. Listen to the material on the audio CD. Repeat these phrases after the speaker.

a)	keep going	h)	get thirsty
b)	big deal	i)	cab driver
c)	look funny	j)	job seeker
d)	stop sign	k)	sad story
e)	get caught	l)	mad money
f)	went down	m)	big storm
g)	walk tall	n)	cold spell

2. Work with a partner. Say the phrases to each other.

3. Choose six phrases from this list and make up a dialogue which you will do for the class.

Condition 3

When a word begins with the same consonant as the previous word ends with, the consonant is pronounced as one slightly longer sound.

 Pronunciation Activity 3

1. Listen to the material on the audio CD. Repeat these phrases after the speaker.

a)	slap Peter	i)	thank Kate
b)	punch Charles	j)	kiss Sue
c)	push Sharon	k)	quiz Zena
d)	hit Terry	l)	tap Paul
e)	kick Catherine	m)	both things
f)	hide Donna	n)	bathe them
g)	hug Gord	o)	dance steps
h)	grab Barbara		

2. Work with a partner. Say the phrases to each other.

3. Choose six sentences from this list and make up a dialogue which you will do for the class.

Pronunciation Activity 4

To practise linking, repeat these phrases after the speaker. Then say them to your partner. Make sure you are linking the words together. Next, choose five to eight phrases from this list and make up a dialogue. Present your dialogue to the class.

1. take off your ring
2. look down
3. look carefree
4. big break
5. big gamble
6. big apple
7. stop it
8. stop people
9. help save
10. job search
11. job benefits
12. job application
13. tried driving
14. tried going
15. tried on the hat
16. got on the bus
17. got scolded
18. got torn
19. other animals
20. black out
21. get over it
22. get away with murder
23. don't put off until tomorrow what you can do today
24. get out of our house

Communicating in the Real World

Try to use your English to talk to people outside your class. Work with a partner to make up a questionnaire asking four to eight questions about one of the following topics. You can ask questions which are similar to the following, or other questions.

Topics: Leisure activities, sports, TV programs, and movies.

1. What is your favourite . . .
2. Why do you like it?
3. When/where do you . . .
4. What is special about . . .
5. When was the last time you . . .
6. Do you think everyone should . . . ? Why or why not?

Show your questions to the teacher. Then find several people outside your class to ask questions. Report what you learned to the class.

Self Evaluation

Rate yourself (using a scale of 0–5, where "5" is the highest ranking) and write your comments in each section of the chart. Show the chart to your teacher and discuss your strengths and weaknesses.

Topic	Good (5, 4)	Improving (3, 2)	Needs more work (1, 0)
Grammar and Language Functions 1. Stating and asking about preferences 2. Expressing ability and inability 3. Expressing advisability and inadvisability 4. Expressing regret, criticizing, and reprimanding 5. Summarizing 6. Expressing possibility/speculating 7. Expressing possibility in the past and speculating about past events			
Speaking Strategies 1. When you are ready to speak, use body language and eye contact to let people know. You can look at the speaker to let her/him know that you are waiting to speak. You can lean forward or lean towards the speaker. 2. When you are ready to speak let the others know by making polite sounds such as: *ah, um, OK,* and *I think . . .* to signal that you are ready to speak. 3. Don't be afraid to try anything to get your message across. You can use pictures, gestures, spelling, or anything else that helps you. 4. What other speaking strategies did you use?			
Listening Strategies 1. It's not necessary to understand every word when you are listening. Focus on the overall meaning when you hear something for the first time. 2. If you can connect the information that you hear in a listening to your own knowledge, experiences, and opinions, you will have a deeper understanding of the information and will be able to evaluate it better. 3. Identify and make a list of words that you do not understand and then find out their meanings. 4. What other listening strategies did you use?			

Topic	Good (5, 4)	Improving (3, 2)	Needs more work (1, 0)
Pronunciation Linking			

Vocabulary and Language Chunks

Write 10 sentences using vocabulary from the chapter.

1. _____
2. _____
3. _____
4. _____
5. _____
6. _____
7. _____
8. _____
9. _____
10. _____

My plan for practising is . . . _____
_____
_____
_____

CHAPTER 6
The Personal and the Professional, Emotions and Work

Thinking and Talking

When dealing with people, you are not dealing with creatures of logic, but creatures of emotion.

—Dale Carnegie

All humanity is passion; without passion, religion, history, novels, art would be ineffectual.

—Honore de Balzac

What do these quotations about emotions mean? Do you agree with them?

Speaking Activity 1

Work in pairs. Interview your partner. Report the most interesting information to the class.

1. Are you an emotional person? When and where do you become emotional?

2. Do you think women are more emotional than men? Why or why not?

3. In your day-to-day activities, is it your head (your mind) or your heart (your feelings) that guides you to make decisions?

4. What do you think the strongest emotions are?

5. In what situations do you think it is important to keep your emotions to yourself?

6. Do people in your country express their emotions more than people in North America? Give some examples.

7. Would you rather fall in love with an emotional person or a rational person? Why?

8. What was the best emotional experience of your life?

9. Tell me about a time you felt proud of yourself.

10. Tell me about a time you felt afraid.

11. Have you ever felt jealous? When and why?

12. Do you ever feel guilty? When and why?

13. Have you ever felt culture shock? Describe how you felt and what happened.

SPEAKING STRATEGY

Use attending behaviours such as looking the speaker in the eye, smiling, nodding, and saying *um*, *uh-uh*, *ah*, *I see*, and *really*. This lets the listener know that you are paying attention, that you are supportive, and it encourages conversation.

Listening 1

Before You Listen

Pre-listening Vocabulary

1. You will hear these words and phrases in the interview you are going to listen to. Work with a partner or by yourself to write the correct vocabulary next to the definitions.

Vocabulary

psychologist	reasoning	jealousy
facial	disgust	pride
Caucasian	distinguish	self-confidence
kinesthetic	primary	universal
pleasure	irritation	marshmallow
multiple	rage	self-awareness
limited	to excel	determination

Definition	Vocabulary
strength of mind and purpose	_____
belief in oneself	_____
knowing oneself	_____
worldwide	_____
a soft, spongy candy	_____
belief in oneself and respect for the value of one's achievements	_____
strong envy	_____
strong anger, fury	_____
annoyance, impatience	_____
first and most important	_____
differentiate, see a difference	_____
aversion, extreme dislike	_____
partial, not completely	_____
do extremely well, to be excellent, to stand out	_____
having to do with bodily movement	_____
thinking, logic, analysis	_____
enjoyment, delight, satisfaction	_____
many, several, more than one	_____
a professional who studies human behaviour	_____
relating to the face	_____
belonging to the light-skinned peoples of Europe and America	_____

2. Work with a small group. Brainstorm all the words dealing with emotions that you can think of. Then put these emotion words into categories. Try to come up with two or more different categories. You could use categories such as positive/negative, and others.

 Listening for the Main Ideas

Listen to the interview on the audio CD once and answer the following questions.

1. Who is Sally Jenkins?

2. What do we find out about emotions?

3. What do we learn about cultural differences?

4. What is the theory of multiple intelligences?

 Listening Comprehension

Listen to the interview again. As you listen, follow the outline of the interview and add any information that is missing.

Pain   Pleasure

1. Interview with Dr. Sally Jenkins

   Profession: psychologist who trains people _____

2. Number and names of emotions identified

   Ekman, Friesen, Ellsworth _____

   Parrot 2001 _____

   Primary emotion—anger; secondary emotions _____

   Primary emotion—joy; secondary emotions _____

3. Research—cultural differences in recognizing emotions in facial expressions.

   Results show _____

4. Emotional intelligence

   Definition_____

5. Multiple intelligences

   Gardiner developed theory of
   multiple intelligences because _____

6. Definitions of multiple intelligences

   Verbal-linguistic intelligence _____

   Logical-mathematical intelligence _____

   Visual-spatial intelligence_____

   Bodily-kinesthetic intelligence _____

   Musical intelligence_____

   Interpersonal intelligence_____

   Intrapersonal intelligence_____

   Naturalist intelligence _____

   Emotional intelligence is a combination of _____

 LISTENING STRATEGY

Paying attention to details can give you a clearer picture of the overall message.

7. Examples of emotional intelligence:

Marshmallow study _____

J.K. Rowling, author of the Harry Potter books _____

8. How emotional intelligence can help in
language learning _____

Personalizing

Work with a group. Discuss the following statements from the interview. Try to
reach consensus and then present your ideas to the rest of the class.

Statements	Agree	Disagree	Reasons
The expression of emotions is different in different cultures.	_____	_____	_____
A very important part of learning a language is learning what words and what body language to use to express feelings.	_____	_____	_____
The traditional idea of intelligence doesn't explain why people have such different abilities.	_____	_____	_____
Emotional intelligence, more than anything, else is responsible for success in business and in life.	_____	_____	_____

Vocabulary and Language Chunks

Write the number of the expression next to the meaning. After checking your
answers, choose six expressions and write your own sentences.

Expressions

1. to make sense
2. no matter
3. to do a study
4. to make errors
5. to pay attention to
6. wide range of
7. to see eye to eye
8. eye-opening
9. capable of
10. in (my) case
11. to have no idea
12. to carry on
13. over time

Meanings

[ ] in (my) example

[ ] to be able to do something

[ ] to agree

[ ] to do research

[ ] to make mistakes

[ ] regardless, irrespective, it doesn't matter

[ ] revealing, enlightening

[ ] to continue on

[ ] not to know

[ ] to be understandable, to be logical, coherent

[ ] to focus on, be attentive to

[ ] over a period of time

[ ] a great variety of

SPEAKING STRATEGY

When answering questions, do not wait for longer than a few seconds before saying something. Even if you are not ready to answer, acknowledge the question by saying something like *ummm*, *ah*, *OK*, or something like "I'm still thinking about that," "That's a difficult question," "I'm not quite sure what I think," or "Let me think."

Communication Focus: Expressing Assumptions and Expressing Probability

When we make assumptions, we are saying that we are 80 per cent or 90 per cent sure of something. There are forms for expressing assumptions or probability in the affirmative and the negative, but there is no question form.

Structures/Expressions	Examples
. . . must + the base form of the verb	Jake always bites his nails. He must be nervous.
	Jean and Fred are always together and holding hands. They must care about each other.
. . . probably . . .	Jake is probably nervous.
	Jean and Fred probably care about each other.
. . . assume . . .	I assume Jake is nervous.
	I assume Jean and Fred care about each other.

Communication Focus: Expressing Negative Probability and Assumptions

Structures/Expressions	Examples
. . . can't + the base form of the verb . . . couldn't + the base form of the verb	1. She never eats pasta. She can't like it very much. She couldn't like it very much.
. . . mustn't + the base form of the verb (this is used mostly in spoken English)	She mustn't like it very much.
	2. He works part time. He can't make a lot of money. He couldn't make a lot of money. He mustn't make a lot of money.
. . . probably not . . .	She probably doesn't like pasta. He probably doesn't make a lot of money.
. . . assume . . .	I assume she doesn't like pasta. I assume he doesn't make a lot of money.

Speaking Activity 2

Work with a partner. Answer these questions about the listening exercise on the audio CD using modals of *probability* or *possibility*.

1. Why don't the psychologists agree about how many emotions there are?

2. Why is it difficult for East Asians to recognize some of the facial expressions of Westerners?

3. Why do people differ so much in the things they can do?

4. If someone is very good at math and reaching logical conclusions, what kind of intelligence can we assume he or she has?

5. If someone learns best when she or he can move around the room or go on field trips, what kind of intelligence does the person probably have?

6. If someone gets along well with everybody, what can we say about that person's strengths?

7. English teachers are usually really good at using language. What can we say about their strengths?

8. What do you think people who have high levels of emotional intelligence are good at?

Speaking Activity 3

Work in groups of three. Discuss several things that you are each good at doing, and some that you are not very good at doing. Then decide on two intelligences you must be strong in and two that you are probably weak in.

	Skills	Not Very Good At	Intelligences/ Strengths	Intelligences/ Weaknesses
Partner #1	_____	_____	_____	_____
	_____	_____	_____	_____
Partner #2	_____	_____	_____	_____
	_____	_____	_____	_____
Partner #3	_____	_____	_____	_____

Speaking Activity 4

Work with a partner. State one affirmative and one negative assumption about people in your class or about famous people you have seen in the news. Give reasons for your assumptions.

Name	Affirmative	Negative
1. _____	_____	_____
	_____	_____
2. _____	_____	_____
	_____	_____
3. _____	_____	_____
	_____	_____
4. _____	_____	_____
	_____	_____

Communication Focus: Expressing Assumptions and Probability in the Past

When we want to express 80–90 per cent certainty in the past, we use the following structures and expressions. As in the present, there are structures for expressing probability in the affirmative and negative, but there is no question form.

Structures/Expressions	Examples
Must + have + past participle	Jane and Larry won the ice dancing competition. They must have practised a lot.
Negative: couldn't/can't + have + past participle of the verb	Ellen failed the exam. She couldn't/can't have studied a lot.
Probably	They probably practised a lot.
Negative: probably not	Ellen failed the exam. She probably didn't study.

 Please go to the website for more practice with this structure.

Speaking Activity 5

Work with a partner. Express assumptions in the past about the following famous personalities.

1. Michael Shumacher (famous Formula 1 race car driver)
2. Michael Jordan (basketball player)
3. Mike Weir (golfer)
4. Pele (the most famous Brazilian soccer player)
5. Wayne Gretzky (famous Canadian hockey player)
6. Serena Williams (famous American tennis player)
7. Madonna (American singer, entertainer)
8. Celine Dion (Canadian singer, entertainer)

Communication Focus: Expressing Emotions

The following are some expressions for expressing the emotions of fear, worry, anger, love, and joy. Supply two examples for each emotion. These can be about yourself or a classmate. Share your examples with the class.

Fear

Structures/Expressions	Examples
. . . to be afraid of . . .	_____
. . . to be frightened of . . .	_____
. . . to be scared of . . .	_____
. . . to be terrified of . . .	_____

Worry

Structures/Expressions	Examples
. . . to be worried about . . .	_____
. . . to be nervous about . . .	_____
. . . to be anxious about . . .	_____
. . . to be uneasy about . . .	_____
. . . to be apprehensive about . . .	_____

Anger

Structures/Expressions	**Examples**
. . . to be angry at/about . . .	_____
. . . to be furious at/about . . .	_____
. . . to be exasperated at/by . . .	_____
. . . to be irritated by . . .	_____
. . . to be frustrated by . . .	_____
. . . to be annoyed by . . .	_____

Love

Structures/Expressions	**Examples**
. . . to love . . .	_____
. . . to adore . . .	_____
. . . to be fond of . . .	_____
. . . to feel affection for . . .	_____

Joy/Pleasure

Structures/Expressions	**Examples**
. . . to be happy/pleased about . . .	_____
. . . to be delighted about . . .	_____
. . . to be thrilled about/by . . .	_____
. . . to be ecstatic about . . .	_____

Speaking Activity 6

Work in groups of five. Each person should choose one of the five questions below and speak first to the others in the group, and then to all the others in the class, asking their question. When you are answering questions, use the expressions for expressing emotions.

When everyone has finished, regroup into five large groups, so that all the A's, B's, C's, D's, and E's are together. As a group, put together a class profile based on the information that you found out about fears, worries, etc. Create a chart or a graph and choose someone from each of the groups to report to the class.

A. What are you most afraid/frightened of?

B. What are you worried/nervous/uneasy about?

C. What are you angry/irritated/annoyed about?

D. What are you fond of/feel affection for?

E. What are you delighted/thrilled about?

Speaking Activity 7

In February 2001, a poll was conducted among over 1,000 North Americans. They were asked the question "What are you afraid of most?" They listed the following fears. Work with a partner to guess the order of the fears.

Rank "1" for the most common fear, "2" for the second most common, and so on. When you have finished, check the Answer Key to find out what the results were.

Fears	Rank
Going to the doctor	_____
Fear of crowds	_____
Heights	_____
Being in an enclosed small space	_____
Thunder and lightning	_____
Flying on a plane	_____
Dogs	_____
Mice	_____
Snakes	_____
Speaking in public	_____
Spiders and insects	_____
Needles and getting shots	_____

What do you think the top ten fears might be today? Try to explain the reasons for differences

Communication Focus: Making and Responding to Suggestions

Suggestions are less forceful and less direct than advice. We make suggestions to friends, colleagues, and others who have indicated a problem.

Structures/Expressions	Examples
Have you thought of . . .	Have you thought of trying to be friendlier?
You might . . .	You might try to be friendlier.
You could . . .	You could try to be friendlier.
Why don't you . . .	Why don't you try to be friendlier?
How about . . .	How about trying to be friendlier?
What about . . .	What about trying to be friendlier?

Responses

Positive	Negative
You're right. I should try that.	I'm not sure that's a good idea.
You think so? I'll try that. Thanks.	I don't know about that.
I suppose/guess I should . . .	I don't think that will work.
That's a good/great idea. I'll try it.	That's not me. I couldn't/can't do that.
Maybe you're right. I'll give it a try.	

Speaking Activity 8

The following are some problems that people face when learning a new language. Work with a partner. Choose two problems and develop a dialogue for each. Use expressions for making and responding to suggestions. Role-play your best dialogue for the class.

1. I am afraid to speak English on the phone.

2. I am anxious about making mistakes and I can't say anything.

3. I am very nervous about speaking to native speakers. I might not understand them and they probably won't understand me.

4. I am scared to death of looking stupid because I can't say what I mean in English.

5. I am irritated at not having enough words to express my ideas.

6. English grammar drives me crazy! I can never remember the rules!

7. I am frustrated because whenever I try to say something, no one is able to understand me. It must be my pronunciation.

8. I am frustrated because often when I am listening to someone speak English, I can't understand what they are saying.

Speaking Activity 9

Work with a partner. Here is a list of emotions. What adjectives do we use to describe people who are feeling that emotion? Write out the adjective forms. Rate the emotions as strengths or weaknesses. Then develop a dialogue with your partner. Tell each other about two of your weaknesses. Make suggestions to each other to overcome these.

Sample dialogue

You: One of my weaknesses is that I get angry easily. I lose my temper. I can't control my anger.

Your Partner: Have you thought of taking a deep breath before you say anything when you are angry? That works for me.

You: That's a good idea. I'll try it.

Emotion Noun	Descriptive Adjective	Strength or Weakness
Homesickness		
Happiness		
Love		
Jealousy		
Anger		
Sadness		
Hate		
Irritation		
Delight		
Fury		
Apprehension		
Pride		
Self-confidence		
Loneliness		
Fear		
Motivation		
Determination		

Speaking Activity 10

Take this self-esteem test by yourself. This test measures overall self-esteem and it is used by psychologists. When you have finished, compare your score with a partner's. Give each other suggestions for improving your self-esteem.

Questions	Strongly Agree	Agree	Disagree	Strongly Disagree
1. On the whole, I am satisfied with myself.				
2. At times, I think I am no good at all.				
3. I feel that I have a number of good qualities.				
4. I am able to do things as well as most other people.				
5. I feel I do not have much to be proud of.				
6. I certainly feel useless at times.				
7. I feel that I'm a person of worth, at least equal to others.				
8. I wish I could have more respect for myself.				
9. All in all, I am inclined to feel that I am a failure.				
10. I take a positive attitude toward myself.				

Scoring: For questions 1, 3, 4, 7, 10 score in the following way: SA=3, A=2, D=1, SD=0. For questions 2, 5, 6, 8, 9 score: SA=0, A=1, D=2, SD=3. Add up the scores for the 10 items. The higher the score, the higher the self-esteem. Scores below 15 suggest low self-esteem.

Speaking Activity 11

Work in groups of three or four. Discuss the following questions with the people in your group.

1. Are you a superstitious person? Do you believe in good luck and bad luck? Why or why not?
2. Are people from your country or city usually superstitious?
3. What are some lucky numbers or unlucky numbers?
4. Do you know any superstitions about animals?
5. Do you know any superstitions about plants or flowers?
6. Do you know any superstitions about love and marriage?
7. What are some other superstitions from your country?

8. What North American superstitions do you know?

9. Are the following good luck or bad luck?

   a)   You break a mirror.

   b)   You open an umbrella inside the house.

   c)   You see a rainbow.

   d)   You find a horseshoe.

   e)   You see a black cat.

   f)   You walk under a ladder.

Communication Focus: Apologizing and Responding

An apology in English can have five distinct features. For a minor offence, such as stepping on someone's toe or bumping into someone, we use only an expression of regret. It's not necessary to give an explanation. In other cases, English speakers use an expression of regret and an explanation, and some other elements depending on how serious the offence is, the relationship of the speakers, and the context.

Features of an Apology	Examples
1. Expression of regret	I am (really) (very) (awfully) sorry. I apologize. I owe you an apology. Please forgive me for . . . Excuse me . . .* Pardon me . . .*
2. Acknowledgement of responsibility	It's my fault . . . I broke the glass. I lost your book.
3. Explanation or account of what happened	The glass slipped . . . I forgot . . . My car broke down . . . I wasn't thinking . . . I didn't see you . . .
4. Offer of repair	Let me get you a new one. Could we reschedule . . . How can I make it up to you?
5. Promise of non-recurrence	I'll be more careful next time. It won't happen again.

* These phrases are used for very minor offences.

Formal Responses to an Apology

Positive	Negative
That's all right.	I'm sorry, an apology isn't enough.
Please don't worry about it.	I don't think I can accept your apology.
I accept your apology.	
It's not important.	I am afraid an apology isn't enough.

Less Formal Responses to an Apology

Positive	Negative
You couldn't help it.	It's not OK.
It wasn't your fault.	You did it on purpose.
That's OK.	
No problem.	
No worries!	

Speaking Activity 12

Work with a partner. Compare apologies in other countries with English apologies. How are the apologies the same? How are they different?

Apologies in English	Apologies in _____	Apologies in _____
1. Expression of regret	YES / NO How is it different? _____	YES / NO How is it different? _____
2. Acknowledgement of responsibility	_____	_____
3. Explanation or account of what happened	_____ _____ _____ _____	_____ _____ _____ _____
4. Offer of repair	_____	_____
5. Promise of non-recurrence	_____	_____

Speaking Activity 13

Work with a small group. Talk about the last time you each apologized. What happened? Who did you apologize to? Where were you? What did you say?

Name	Reason for Apology	Who Did You Apologize To?	Where?	What Did You Say?
_____	_____	_____	_____	_____
_____	_____	_____	_____	_____
_____	_____	_____	_____	_____
_____	_____	_____	_____	_____
_____	_____	_____	_____	_____

Speaking Activity 14

Work with a partner. Some of the following are expressions of regret (apologies). Others are responses to apologies. Complete the dialogues by writing a response or an apology as required.

1. a) I'm terribly sorry I'm late. My bus didn't come on time.

   b) _____

2. a) I owe you an apology. I still haven't returned the book I borrowed three weeks ago. I keep forgetting to bring it to class.

   b) _____

3. a) I have to apologize for mispronouncing your name. I'm just not good at remembering how to pronounce unusual names. Sorry.

   b) _____

4. a) Please forgive me for spilling coffee on you. I hope you're OK. You know, I am one of the clumsiest people around!

   b) _____

5. a) Sorry I slammed the door. I didn't realize you were behind me.

   b) _____

6. a) I'm sorry I am going to miss your presentation. I have to leave early because I have a dental appointment.

   b) _____

7. a) _____

   b) It's all right this time, but please make sure it doesn't happen again.

8. a) _____

   b) That's all right. I understand. I'll make sure to tell you about the next one.

9. a) _____

   b) OK. I hope it doesn't become a habit!

10. a) _____

    b) I'm afraid I can't accept your apology. This is a serious issue.

11. a) _____

    b) Don't worry about it. I know you didn't do it on purpose.

12. a) _____

    b) That's OK. It wasn't your fault.

Speaking Activity 15

Work with a partner. Examine the apologies and responses. Decide if they are appropriate or not. Explain your decisions.

1. John: Have you seen my camera?

   Liang: I left it in the restaurant, sorry.

2. Eric: What happened to the front bumper?

   Kassia: I hit a fire hydrant. I didn't even see it. Sorry.

3. Maja: Oh no, look at my white shag carpet! What happened?

   Irina: My boyfriend spilled a bottle of red wine. I'll clean it up. Don't worry.

4. Fred: Do you realize what time it is? You're more than an hour late!

   Akiko: I was held up at the meeting. Hope you don't mind.

5. Jane: It was my birthday last week.

   Marcel: It was? I'm so sorry, I forgot. I've had so much on my mind recently. Please forgive me. Let me make it up by taking you out for dinner.

Speaking Activity 16

Work with a partner. In each of the apologies below, what do you think the relationship of the speakers might be? What do you think the offence could be, and how serious do you think it is? Role-play two apologies.

1. a) Sorry about that!　　　　　　　　　b) No worries!

Offence	Relationship	Seriousness
_____	_____	_____
_____	_____	_____

2. a) Sorry I forgot to call you last night.　　　b) No problem. I was really busy finishing my assignment.

Offence	Relationship	Seriousness
_____	_____	_____
_____	_____	_____

3. a) I'm terribly sorry I missed the meeting this morning. There was a bad accident on the expressway and I was stuck in traffic for an hour.

   b) OK, but we have to get together to discuss this project.

   a) Could we possibly meet tomorrow morning?

   b) All right. Let's try for tomorrow morning. Same time, same place?

   a) Sure and I apologize again for this morning. I promise it won't happen again.

Offence	Relationship	Seriousness
_____	_____	_____
_____	_____	_____

4. a) I'm really sorry but I won't be able to hand in my essay tomorrow. My parents just arrived in town and I have to spend some time with them tonight. I'll try to hand it in, in a couple of days.

   b) I am afraid that won't do. I'll have to deduct marks. You have had a few weeks to do this assignment.

   a) Yeah, I know. I'll try to have it in as soon as I can. If I give it to you in two days, how will that affect my mark?

   b) Well, if you get it in by Friday, you'll only lose five marks.

   a) OK. That's not too bad. Thanks for being so understanding. I promise this won't happen again.

Offence	Relationship	Seriousness
_____	_____	_____
_____	_____	_____

Speaking Activity 17

Work with a partner. Choose three situations and role-play apologizing and responding to apologies. Use the apology checklist as you listen to your classmates' apology role-plays.

1. You borrowed your friend's favourite sweater and you can't remember where you left it.
2. You missed a test. You had a terrible migraine headache.
3. You couldn't go out for your friend's birthday because your boyfriend/ girlfriend had gotten tickets for a concert on that day.
4. You missed your appointment with the counsellor because you had to take a sick friend to the hospital.
5. You borrowed your friend's laptop and now it doesn't work any more.
6. You spilled red wine on your teacher's cream-coloured carpet.

Apology Checklist	YES/NO	Comments
Expression of regret		
Acknowledgement of responsibility		
Explanation		
Offer of repair		
Promise of non-recurrence		
Formality		
Politeness		

Speaking Activity 18

The following is a list of real but unusual jobs. Can you guess what these professionals do? Choose the correct answer. Compare your answers with a partner and then tell each other about the most unusual jobs you have ever had.

1. Laughter therapists ...
   a) like to laugh.
   b) laugh for a living.
   c) encourage people to think happy thoughts and make them laugh because laughter is good for circulation, mental health, and spiritual well being.

2. Vermiculturists ...
   a) study culture for a living.
   b) farm worms. (Worms are a good way of decomposing rotten material and are environmentally friendly.)
   c) work in a beauty salon.

3. Storm chasers ...
   a) follow and record storms to study weather patterns.
   b) chase police cars.
   c) work in a water treatment plant.

4. Subway crowd pushers ...
   a) sell subway tickets to large groups.
   b) beg for money on subway trains.
   c) try to fit more people into already crowded subway cars.

5. Food stylists ...
   a) style hair in a supermarket.
   b) style hair for wedding parties and banquets.
   c) arrange and style food in magazine ads, movies, and TV.

6. Pet sitters ...
   a) care for pets when owners are away.
   b) teach pets tricks such as sitting up.
   c) teach pets discipline.

7. Acupuncturists ...
   a) punch holes in papers.
   b) put needles into patients to cure them.
   c) drill holes for pipes accurately.

8. Master sniffers ...
   a) smell things for a living.
   b) own big dogs.
   c) train animals to track smells.

Please check your answers in the Answer Key.

Listening 2

Before You Listen

Pre-listening Vocabulary

1. You will hear these words and phrases in the panel discussion you are going to listen to. Work with a partner or by yourself to write the correct vocabulary next to the definitions.

Vocabulary

maximize	rapid	author	profitable
atmosphere	obstacle	lap	inspiring
coach	to impact	role model	upbeat
unique	access	mentor	
downsize	counsellor	to pursue	
resistance	statistics	achievable	

Definition	Vocabulary
guide, advisor, tutor, a person who helps another to achieve success	_____
data, information, numbers	_____
mood, feeling, ambiance	_____
the right to enter, admittance	_____
barrier, obstruction, blockage	_____
only one of its kind	_____
to follow, chase after	_____
to make the best use of, make the most of	_____
trainer, teacher, instructor, one who coaches	_____
to cut back, scale back, make smaller	_____
writer	_____
very fast	_____
to have a strong influence, effect on	_____
someone who advises, helps with problems	_____
someone a person chooses to imitate	_____
opposition	_____
the upper leg area when a person is seated	_____
reachable, doable	_____
making money, making a profit	_____
happy, optimistic, cheerful	_____
giving feelings of positive emotions and confidence	_____

2. Work with a partner. Brainstorm all the words that come to mind under the heading "The Best Jobs in the World."

Listening for the Main Ideas

Listen to the interview on the audio CD once. Write YES next to the topics that are discussed by the panel.

1. The impact of technology

2. When is the best time to start working towards finding a dream job

3. The sooner a person can figure out what her dream job is, the better

4. Dreams come in all shapes and sizes

5. The practical steps to take in looking for dream jobs

6. Barbara Sher's book, *Live the Life You Love*

7. Success stories about jobs

LISTENING STRATEGY

Try to identify key words, which are the important words often repeated throughout a text. This will help you understand what the listening is about.

 Listening Comprehension

Listen to the panel discussion again. As you listen, write TRUE or FALSE next to each sentence. Please listen to the discussion again if necessary.

1. Martha is a counsellor in a community college who advises students about occupations.

2. Dr James Reynolds has experience only in the business world.

3. Both Melissa and Martha are life coaches.

4. Changes in technology and environmentalism are affecting the work place.

5. Barbara Sher is Melissa Wong's role model.

6. James Reynolds believes it's a good idea to wait for better economic times to look for dream jobs.

7. Martha believes that most people will change jobs several times in their lives.

8. Martha feels that researching careers, employers, and locations gives people a clearer picture of the kind of work they want to do.

9. Melissa Wong believes that people have to discover their special talents first before they can think about what kinds of jobs they should do.

10. Martha says that government research predicts that the most job openings over the next 10 years will be in teaching, accounting auditing, and software engineering.

LISTENING STRATEGY

Evaluate your ability to follow the listening. How well have you understood and been able to follow the main ideas and details?

11. Martha says that the top three occupations for people without university degrees will be in the healthcare field.

12. Melissa Wong thinks that finding one's motivation, gathering a supportive group of people, and overcoming obstacles is the best way to attain one's dream job.

Personalizing

Work with a partner. Ask and answer the following questions. Report the most interesting answers to the class.

1. Which of the three panelists—Melissa, Martha, or James—do you agree with the most? Explain why.

2. What is your dream job? How do you think you could achieve that dream?

3. Do you believe that each of us has a unique talent which makes us special? Explain why or why not.

Vocabulary and Language Chunks

Write the number of the expression next to the meaning. After checking your answers, choose six expressions and write your own sentences.

Expressions

1. overcome obstacles
2. to put off
3. not to get it
4. no point in
5. to grow up
6. to pin down
7. to hang on
8. to make someone's day
9. to get someone going
10. to have a chance
11. to get pumped up
12. to make a point
13. to land a job

Meanings

☐ no reason to

☐ to wait a moment

☐ to make someone very happy,, to provide the best point in a person's day

☐ not to understand

☐ to master, surmount something that blocks the way

☐ to make someone excited, ready to work

☐ to postpone, delay

☐ mature, become an adult

☐ to state a valid argument

☐ to get very excited, enthusiastic

☐ to pinpoint, clarify

☐ to get a job

☐ to have the opportunity

Communication Focus: Giving Complex Descriptions

We can use an adjective clause to describe a noun or pronoun, and in this way provide a more complex description.

Examples

A life coach is a person *who advises and helps clients reach their goals.*
If you find a job *which you enjoy*, you will never work a day in your life.

Grammar Note

Who, whom*, *that*, and *whose* introduce relative clauses referring to people.

Examples

The woman **who (or that)** lives next door is a professor.
The man **whom (or that) (or no relative pronoun******)** you talked to, used to be an accountant.
The man **whose** wife is the CEO of the company has retired.

Examples

Which and *that* introduce relative clauses referring to things.
The occupations **which (or that)** will have the most openings in the next ten years are in the computer and health care fields.
The course **that (or which) (or no relative pronoun*****)** you need to take runs in the evenings.

*The use of *whom* is rare in conversation or writing.

**When the relative pronoun can be left out, leave it out. This is the most common in speaking and writing.

Speaking Activity 19

Work with a partner. Give definitions of the following professions. Use relative clauses. When you have finished, think of five additional occupations. Share your information with the class.

Example

An interviewer is a person who interviews people on television or radio. An interviewer may also be someone who interviews people for jobs.

1. panelist
2. author
3. counsellor
4. interpreter
5. auditor
6. software engineer
7. lawyer
8. winemaker
9. server
10. novelist
11. designer
12. dolphin trainer

Speaking Activity 20

Work in groups of four. Decide as a group which two jobs (of any jobs that you can think of) are the most exciting, the most dangerous, the most unpleasant, the most important, and the most highly paid. Give reasons for your choices.

The Most Exciting Jobs	The Most Dangerous Jobs	The Most Unpleasant Jobs	The Most Important Jobs	The Most Highly Paid Jobs
_____	_____	_____	_____	_____
_____	_____	_____	_____	_____
_____	_____	_____	_____	_____

Speaking Activity 21

Work in groups of three. Explain what the following objects are and what they do. Use relative clauses. If you aren't sure, guess. Try to come up with two more of your own. Then check your answers with another group.

Example

A can opener is a tool which we use to open cans with.

Item	Answer/Guess	Correct?
1. a folder	_____	_____
2. a blender	_____	_____
3. a bestseller	_____	_____
4. a money-maker	_____	_____
5. a lawn mower	_____	_____
6. a tear jerker	_____	_____
7. a toaster	_____	_____
8. a stroller	_____	_____
9. a password	_____	_____
10. a peep hole	_____	_____
11.	_____	_____
12.	_____	_____

Communication Focus: Adding Information and Ideas

These expressions add information and ideas, and may help to keep a conversation going.

Structures/Expressions

I'd like to add . . .

What's more . . .

Furthermore . . .

Yes, and to take that a little further . . .

And besides that . . .

And in addition . . .*

And moreover . . .*

*And in addition . . . and And moreover . . . are used mostly in writing; they are very formal sounding in speaking.

Speaking Activity 22

Work in pairs. Interview your partner about work. Use expressions to add information and ideas. Report to the class on the most interesting information you found out.

1. What is your dream job? Why?

2. What's your idea of a terrible job?

3. Would you rather work for a male boss or a female boss?

4. What do you think is the best way to find a job?

5. If you didn't have to work, would you? Why?

6. What kind of work do you think you will be doing 10 years from now?

7. What is more important—making a lot of money or really enjoying your job?

8. How many careers or occupations do you think you will have in your life time?

9. Do you think there is equal opportunity for everyone in the work place? Why?

10. What do you think about self-employment or freelancing as ways of earning a living?

Speaking Activity 23

Work with a partner. Decide on a definition of a workaholic. Then, take the following test. Answer the questions with YES or NO. Compare your answers with your partner. Do you think you are a workaholic? Check the Answer Key.

1. Are you usually unable to finish your daily to-do list?

2. Are you unhappy with your work/life balance?

3. Do you work more hours than others in your area?

4. Working more doesn't give you a sense of satisfaction.

5. Do you feel stressed in your daily life?

6. Do you feel you are stuck in a routine?

7. Do you have an exaggerated sense of the importance of work in your life?

8. Do you find it impossible to finish your work on time?

9. Do you feel guilty if you are not working?

10. Do you take phone calls or work on your breaks?

11. Do you work through lunch or have lunch at your desk?

12. Do you avoid delegating work because you feel you are the only one who can do it?

13. Are you unwilling to take vacations because you fear falling behind in your work or that your job will be gone when you come back?

Communication Focus: Describing Skills, Knowledge, and Abilities

In addition to *can/could/be able to*, there are other ways of describing skills, knowledge, and abilities.

Structures/Expressions	Examples
. . . know how to . . .	She knows how to drive a truck.
. . . understand when to . . .	They understand when to turn the fan on.
. . . study what to . . .	She studied what to do in an emergency.
. . . learn where to . . .	He learned where to find the biggest fish.
. . . discover how long to . . .	She discovered how long to run the program.

Speaking Activity 24

Work in groups of four. Each person should think of two things they know how to do very well and two things they would like to learn how to do. Find out about each other. Make suggestions about how to learn to do the activities mentioned by the group.

Name	Knows How To...	Wants to Learn...	Suggestions

Speaking Activity 25

Work with a partner and choose a profession from the list. Decide what people in the profession you chose know/understand/have learned. Think of unusual activities. When it is your turn, both of you will give the class a description of the profession you chose, without stating the name of the profession. For example, say this is a person who knows/understands/has learned how to . . . /when to . . . /where to. . . . The class takes turns guessing. The people who guess the profession correctly take the next turn.

Professions/Occupations

Software engineer	Archaeologist	Orderly	Interior designer
Coach	Accountant	Plumber	Ambulance
Chef	Undertaker	Mechanic	attendant
Pharmacist	Nurse	Beautician	Linguist
ESL teacher	Architect	Surgeon	

Communication Focus: Interrupting

In the give and take of normal conversation, people may interrupt each other. It's important to use structures or expressions to let others know that you want to interrupt.

Structures/Expressions

Excuse me, may (can) I interrupt?

Pardon me, I'd like to say something.

Would you allow me to interrupt (say something)?

Do you mind if I interrupt?

Can (could) I jump in here?

Hang on. I'd like to say (add) something.

Speaking Activity 26

Work in groups of five. Four of you will play the interrupting game and one person will be the score keeper who records the number of interruptions per person. Use two dice. Toss the dice to see who will speak first, second, etc. The first person to speak then tosses the dice. The number that comes up determines the topic. The first person then gives an impromptu talk on that topic for two minutes. The other group members interrupt with valid questions. The person who handles the most interruptions is the winner.

Number	Topic
2	Something I know how to do
3	The easiest job in the world
4	The most difficult job in the world
5	What I would like to learn how to do
6	My strengths—what I am good at
7	My weaknesses
8	Problems in learning English
9	Fears
10	Something that makes me angry
11	What makes me sad
12	The importance of self-confidence and self-esteem

Communication Focus: Restating and Hesitating

When we want to understand what was said, or what is being asked, we can restate the idea to get a clearer understanding of the statement. Restating what you think was said can also provide an opportunity to hesitate and think of an appropriate response.

Structures/Expressions for Restating

So, what you are (he is, they are) saying is . . .

In other words . . .

What you (he/she/they) mean is . . .

If I understand you . . .

Do you mean . . .

Let's put it this way . . .

Structures/Expressions for Hesitating

Well . . . Ah . . . Ummm . . . OK . . .

That's a good point . . . /That's a good question . . .

Let me see . . .

We can use these two communicative functions together. For example, "Well, let me see. So what you are saying is . . . that this job requires special training."

Speaking Activity 27

Work with a partner. Take turns interviewing each other. Use hesitating and restating expressions in your answers.

1. Describe your worst experience at school.
2. What is your long-term career goal?
3. Tell me about a success you experienced.
4. Describe a problem you had and how you solved it.
5. Describe your greatest worry about your future.
6. What do you think your worst habit is?
7. What do you think is unfair in the world of education or work?
8. How does your emotional make up help you or hinder you?

Pronunciation: More on Linking

In normal fast speech in English, we often link the end of one word to the following word. This may cause a change in pronunciation. Pronunciation changes occur under the following conditions.

Condition 1: When a word ending with /t/ is followed by a word beginning with /y/, the resulting sound is pronounced /tʃ/ as in <u>ch</u>ur<u>ch</u>.

Pronunciation Activity 1

Listen to the speaker on the audio CD and write out the sentences you hear.
Check your work with a partner. Practise repeating the sentences to each other.

1. _____
2. _____
3. _____
4. _____
5. _____
6. _____
7. _____

8. _____
9. _____
10. _____
11. _____
12. _____
13. _____

Condition 2: When a word ending in /d/ is followed by a word beginning with
/y/, the resulting sound is pronounced as /dʒ/ as in ju<u>dge</u>.

Pronunciation Activity 2

Listen to the speaker on the audio CD and write out the sentences you hear.
Check you work with a partner, then repeat the sentences to each other.

1. _____
2. _____
3. _____
4. _____
5. _____
6. _____
7. _____

8. _____
9. _____
10. _____
11. _____
12. _____
13. _____
14. _____

Pronunciation Activity 3

Work with a partner. Make up questions for the answers using phrases with /tʃ/
or /dʒ/. Then practise saying them.

1. _____?
   I bought this dress at a flea market.

2. _____?
   I came here in 2008.

3. _____?
   I put my hat on the shelf.

4. _____?
   I met that young woman in an English class.

5. _____?
   No, I ate breakfast this morning.

6. _____?
   As a matter of fact, I didn't like the play at all.

7. _____?
   Sure. I'd be happy to sit down.

8. _____?
   I took a cab.

9. _____?
   I went to the library and I went alone.

10. _____?
    I called you at seven o'clock because I wanted
    your help.

Pronunciation Activity 4

Work with a partner. Make up a dialogue using as many phrases with /tʃ/ or /dʒ/ as you can. Your dialogue should be logical and natural sounding.

Condition 3: When a tense vowel is followed by a word that begins with a vowel, the words are linked by the semi-vowels /y/ or /w/.

 ## Pronunciation Activity 5

Listen to the speaker on the audio CD say these phrases. Write the sentences and the sound you hear linking the words. Then, listen a second time and repeat the phrases.

1. Do it (w)
2. See Ann (y)
3. _____
4. _____
5. _____
6. _____

7. _____
8. _____
9. _____
10. _____
11. _____
12. _____

 ## Pronunciation Activity 6

Repeat the following sentences after the speaker on the audio CD. Then practise them again with a partner.

1. Did you buy it?
2. When did you see it?
3. How can you do it?
4. Go ahead.
5. Can I try it?
6. How much did you pay her?
7. She must be at home.
8. There's no answer.
9. You know it's time for the meeting.
10. Oh, I totally forgot.
11. You really ought to write things down.
12. Oh, I can't be bothered.
13. You should try it. It'll grow on you.
14. Why are you giving me such a hard time?
15. Sorry. I won't do it again.

Condition 4: When a tense vowel is followed by a word which begins with a semi-vowel (w, y), the semi-vowel is pronounced as one long sound.

Pronunciation Activity 7

Listen to the speaker on the audio CD say these phrases. Repeat the phrases after the speaker and then practise saying them with a partner.

1. Be young
2. Free university
3. Say yes
4. Go where

5. Do one
6. See yesterday
7. Blue water
8. Try yellow

Pronunciation Activity 8

Make up five dialogues using as many of all of the above as you can.

 Pronunciation Activity 9

It's important for English learners to understand reductions, but you do not have to try to speak that way yourself. Listen to the speaker on the audio CD and write out the sentences that you hear. Then check your sentences with a partner.

1. _____
2. _____
3. _____
4. _____
5. _____
6. _____
7. _____
8. _____
9. _____
10. _____
11. _____
12. _____
13. _____
14. _____
15. _____

Communicating in the Real World

Try to use your English to talk to people outside your class. Work with a partner to make up a questionnaire asking four to eight questions about one of the following topics. Show your questions to the teacher. Then speak to one or more people who are not in your class and report to the class what you learned.

Topics: emotions, intelligence/multiple intelligences, fears/worries, jobs/employment/work/skills, dream jobs

Self Evaluation

Rate yourself (using a scale of 0–5, where "5" is the highest ranking) and write your comments in each section of the chart. Show the chart to your teacher and discuss your strengths and weaknesses.

Topic	Good (5, 4)	Improving (3, 2)	Needs more work (1, 0)
Grammar and Language Functions 1. Expressing assumptions and probability 2. Expressing assumptions and probability in the past 3. Expressing emotions 4. Apologizing and responding to apologies 5. Giving complex descriptions 6. Adding information and ideas 7. Describing skills, knowledge, and abilities 8. Interrupting 9. Restating and hesitating			
Speaking Strategies 1. Use attending behaviours such as looking the speaker in the eye, smiling and nodding, and saying *um, uhuh, ah,* and *I see.* This lets the listener know you are supportive, that you are paying attention, and encourages conversation. 2. When answering questions, do not wait for longer than three or four seconds before saying something. Even if you are not ready to answer, acknowledge the question by saying something like *ummm, ah, OK,* or something like "I'm still thinking about that," "That's a difficult question," or "I'm not quite sure what I think." 3. What other speaking strategies did you use?			
Listening Strategies 1. Paying attention to the details can give you a clearer picture of the general ideas and overall message. 2. Try to identify key words, the important words which are often repeated throughout a text. This will help you understand what the listening is about. 3. Evaluate your ability to follow the listening. How well have you understood and been able to follow the main ideas and details? 4. What other strategies did you use?			

Topic	Good (5, 4)	Improving (3, 2)	Needs more work (1, 0)
Pronunciation More on linking			

Vocabulary and Language Chunks

Write 10 sentences using vocabulary from the chapter.

1. _____
2. _____
3. _____
4. _____
5. _____
6. _____
7. _____
8. _____
9. _____
10. _____

My plan for practising is . . . _____

_____

_____

_____

CHAPTER 7
Society and Culture

Thinking and Talking

Do this quiz about gestures around the world. Compare your answers with a partner.

1. The OK gesture is considered _____ .
   a) rude in Brazil
   b) rude in England
   c) rude in Canada and the USA

2. Pulling down the far corner of your eye with the index or middle finger in France means _____ .
   a) I like looking at you
   b) I am going to cry
   c) I do not believe you

3. Curling your index finger towards you to summon someone is _____ .
   a) very insulting in some Asian countries
   b) a compliment in Singapore
   c) not polite in North America

4. Standing with hands on the hips is an expression of _____ .
   a) openness and self-confidence in North America
   b) hostility in Mexico
   c) both of the above

5. The thumbs-up gesture signals _____ .
   a) all is well/very good in Iran
   b) all is well/very good in North America
   c) a polite gesture in some Middle Eastern countries

6. If you sit with the soles of your feet or shoes showing you will insult _____ .
   a) people from some Middle Eastern countries
   b) people from Thailand
   c) both of the above

7. Tipping the head backwards and making a clicking sound with the tongue means _____ .

    a) "no" to people from Saudi Arabia and other Middle Eastern countries

    b) "Let's have a drink" to people from Finland

    c) "Good job" to people from Europe

8. Men holding hands as they walk and talk is considered _____ .

    a) normal, friendly behaviour for males in Spain or South America

    b) normal, friendly behaviour for males in the USA and Canada

    c) normal, friendly behaviour for males in Saudi Arabia

9. Holding the outstretched hand up in front of someone means _____ .

    a) "May I speak?" in some Asian countries

    b) "May I have this dance?" in Argentina

    c) "I don't like you" in Germany

10. Picking one's nose in public is _____ .

    a) a sign that one has a bad cold in Italy

    b) a signal someone is listening to your conversation in South America

    c) not considered particularly rude in China and some other Asian countries

Please check your responses with the Answer Key.

Speaking Activity 1

Work in groups of three. What gestures do people use here and in other countries to send the following messages?

Meaning	Gesture	
	Here	**Other Countries**
to show agreement	_____	_____
to show uncertainty	_____	_____
to get the server's attention in a restaurant	_____	_____
to beckon to someone	_____	_____
to point something out	_____	_____
to get someone to speak louder	_____	_____
to find out if someone is speaking to you	_____	_____
to greet someone	_____	_____
to get someone's attention	_____	_____

Listening 1

Before You Listen

Pre-listening Vocabulary

You will hear these words and phrases in the interview you are going to listen to. Work with a partner or by yourself to write the correct vocabulary next to the definitions.

Vocabulary

taboo	intimidating	limp	to bribe
veteran	nuances	to flash	subtle
to beckon	derogatory	harmless	innocent
globetrotter			

Definition	Vocabulary
world traveller	_____
weak, lacking force	_____
to give money to persuade someone to do something illegal	_____
to send a quick signal	_____
frightening, threatening	_____
slight, delicate, faint	_____
to call someone by a gesture	_____
something forbidden, a prohibition	_____
disrespectful, having a low opinion of	_____
not intended to hurt or harm	_____
without danger or risk	_____
experienced person, old hand	_____
very slight differences, very subtle differences	_____

Listening for the Main Ideas

Listen to the interview on the audio CD once and answer the following questions.

1. What are the main topics in the interview? Put a check next to the main points that the speakers discuss.

   a) books about cultural differences

   b) gestures used in Japan

   c) handshakes in Japan and the Middle East

   d) gestures that fathers teach children

   e) gestures to get attention in a restaurant

   f) gestures that might be rude in some countries but not in others

   g) the universal gesture

2. What is the main idea of this interview?

LISTENING STRATEGY

Try to guess the meaning of phrases you do not understand by using your knowledge of the context and your background knowledge.

Listening Comprehension

Listen to the interview again. The headings below are the most important ideas discussed during the interview. As you listen, take notes about all the details that you hear under each heading. You can listen a second or third time to add more details to your notes. Check your notes with a partner and your teacher.

What to do if you don't understand the language

_____

_____

_____

Roger Axtel

_____

_____

_____

Differences in handshakes

_____

_____

_____

Getting service in a restaurant

_____

_____

_____

The OK gesture

_____

_____

_____

Universally understood gesture

_____

_____

_____

Personalizing

Work in small groups of three or four. Talk about the following topics. Make sure that everyone contributes to the discussion.

1. What new information did you learn from listening to the audio CD?
2. The importance of body language
3. Surprising/unusual North American gestures
4. Surprising/unusual North American customs

SPEAKING STRATEGY

You can paraphrase or use other words to restate your ideas when you think the listeners are not following you. Saying the same thing in a different way can help you to make your ideas clearer, and to make sure that people understand you.

Vocabulary and Language Chunks

Write the number of the expression next to the meaning. After checking your answers, choose six expressions and write your own sentences.

Expressions

1. handy dandy
2. not to work
3. to keep it simple
4. off the top of my head
5. to get someone into trouble
6. to look someone in the eye
7. to catch on
8. back and forth
9. to fall back on
10. to go abroad

Meaning

☐ to resort to, to be able to use in an emergency

☐ to understand, get the message

☐ without thinking too much about something

☐ backwards and forwards, to and fro

☐ to travel to other countries

☐ to put someone into a situation for which they will be criticized, blamed, or punished

☐ to make direct eye contact with someone

☐ to make the message clear, plain, and uncomplicated

☐ not to succeed

☐ convenient, useful, and very good

Communication Focus: Making Recommendations and Predicting Consequences

Here are some structures we can use to make recommendations and to predict the consequences of not following the recommendations.

Structure/Expression	Examples
If . . . will . . .	If you show the soles of your feet in Thailand, you will insult people.
	If you use inappropriate body language, people will think you are rude.
It's (not) a good idea to . . . or (else) . . .	It's not a good idea to burp loudly when you finish your meal or people will think you are rude.
. . . should (not) . . . or (else) . . .	You shouldn't dress too formally for the party or else you'll look out of place.
I recommend . . . or (else) . . .	I recommend not putting your feet up on the table or else you will offend some people.
I recommend/suggest that . . . (This is the most formal usage.)	I recommend that she apologize or else they will be very angry.

Grammar Note

Sentences with if clauses are conditional sentences. In conditional sentences referring to future time, we use the present tense in the if clause. The order of the clauses can be reversed with no change in meaning.

Examples

If you wave at the waiter, you will get his attention.

You'll get the waiter's attention if you wave at him.

Please go to the website for more practice with this structure.

Speaking Activity 2

Work with a partner. Make recommendations and predict consequences in these situations. An example for each situation has been provided.

Eating a meal in a restaurant

Example: You shouldn't drink your soup from your soup bowl or else people will think you are rude.

1. _____
2. _____
3. _____

In a classroom

Example: It's not a good idea to look at another student's work or else the teacher will think you are cheating.

1. _____
2. _____
3. _____

On a bus

Example: If you stare at someone, you will make him or her feel very uncomfortable.

1. _____
2. _____
3. _____

Other situation

1. _____
2. _____
3. _____

Speaking Activity 3

Work in groups of three. What will people think if you do the following in other countries? Tell the country and the consequences of the actions.

1. If you look a teacher or parent directly in the eye
2. If you point at someone or something
3. If you make the OK gesture
4. If you sit on a desk or table
5. If you put your feet on a desk or table
6. If you beckon with your index finger
7. If you leave a party before everyone else
8. If you sit on the floor at a party or gathering

Speaking Activity 4

Work with two partners. One of you will read Article A, the other will read Article B, and the third person will read Article C. Work together to answer the TRUE/FALSE questions and explain what the consequences of inappropriate actions might be (for example, how might people feel and react).

Article A: Eye Contact

"The eyes are the windows to the soul" is a popular North American saying, which tells us that eye contact is of great importance. The right kind of eye contact is part of interacting appropriately in conversation. It is impolite to stare at someone, but it is also impolite not to look at the person at all during conversation. In normal interactions, people look each other in the eye for a few seconds and then gaze away, but they return every few seconds to look the other person in the eye. When you maintain eye contact during a conversation, the speaker usually interprets the eye contact as a sign of interest, confidence, honesty, or sympathy, depending on the type of conversation. If you don't maintain eye contact, people will interpret this as hiding emotions or truth, disagreement, or lack of interest. If a person looks down or looks away during conversation, the signal he or she might be sending is that they are not paying attention or that they are hiding something. This applies to both men and women and to different age groups.

Article B: Space

Did you know that North Americans have a personal space bubble? The personal space that someone needs depends on the situation. When interacting with friends, relatives, or conducting casual business, most people prefer a distance of just over half a meter (almost two feet). When conducting formal or impersonal business, most individuals prefer a personal space of a meter to a meter and a half (about three to five feet). Although the distances for comfortable personal space vary slightly according to the individual, most people will feel that their personal space has been violated if another person sits or stands too close. When personal space is violated, people will feel uncomfortable and may withdraw by backing up or leaving the room. If you notice that others step back from you when speaking, sit at a farther distance, or if they seem physically uncomfortable, they may have a larger personal space need. Have you noticed what happens when North Americans are in small crowded spaces such as elevators or buses? They do not look at each other. People look up; they look down; they read; anything but look at each other. That would be impolite in such close contact.

Article C: Touching Behaviour

Although North Americans are not shy about kissing and embracing their sweethearts or spouses in public, there are some surprising restrictions on touching. For example, friends do not usually kiss each other hello or good-bye, as they do in many other countries. Men and women do not usually walk down the street holding hands with others of the same sex. They don't walk arm-in-arm either. This behaviour is reserved for couples in love. Men rarely touch each other unless they are close family members or friends. An exception might be a man hugging a close friend on greeting or slapping a friend on the back while sharing a joke. Another exception occurs in sports situations. Members of a sports team may touch, slap, or hit each other in the excitement of a game. Men generally greet or say good-bye by shaking hands. Although some young men are beginning to use the bear hug as a greeting, North American men do not hold hands, walk arm-in-arm, or kiss each other in most circumstances. Neither men nor women stand close enough to each other to brush dust or lint off one another. Students would certainly never brush or pick lint off a teacher's clothing or tell a teacher that she has a smudge on her face or clothing.

Statement	TRUE/FALSE	Consequences
If you are friendly and smile, you can look people directly in the eye in elevators.		
It is a sign of respect to look down when an older person is speaking to you.		
If you don't look North Americans in the eye, they will think you are hiding something.		
Staring at someone is considered to be appropriate behaviour during conversation.		
It is important to stand as close as possible to someone when speaking.		
It's OK for young women to hold hands when they are walking down the street.		
It's permissible to give a friend a kiss on the cheek when saying good-bye.		
If your teacher has some dust or dirt on her clothing, it's all right to brush it off.		
If you are paying attention to your friend's story, you can keep looking your friend in the eye.		
You shouldn't ever put your arm around a classmate's shoulders.		
You shouldn't ever kiss someone of the opposite sex in public.		
There's nothing wrong with kissing a very good friend of the same sex on the lips.		
If someone backs away from you during conversation, you should step closer to him or her because they are shy.		

Speaking Activity 5

Customs regarding dating, romance, and marriage differ greatly from culture to culture. Interview a partner and report the most interesting information you learned.

1. How old should young people be in order to date?
2. What do you think the relationship of dating to marriage is?
3. How do people arrange dates in your country? Does the woman or the man do the inviting? Do people go out on "blind dates"?
4. What are the best ways to find a date here?
5. Who should pay for a date?
6. What are the best places to go on a date?
7. What are some wedding customs in your country? Who pays for the wedding? What happens at the celebration?
8. Do men and women behave differently when they are in love?
9. Have you ever been in love? How many times have you been in love? How many times do you think the average person falls in love in a lifetime?
10. Do people look forward to getting married? Why? What is the best age to get married?
11. Describe your ideal partner.
12. Who do you get along better with—men or women?
13. Are there any differences in North America between men and women that you have noticed and that you find interesting?

Communication Focus: Making Complaints

In North American English, speakers can make direct or indirect complaints. The purpose of a direct complaint is to bring about a change. Complaints can have four parts.

Complaint Formula	**Example**
1. Explanation of reason for complaint	I just wanted to see you to talk about my exam.
2. Complaint	In my opinion, my mark was a bit too low.
3. Justification, explanation	I really studied a lot for the exam and I knew all the answers. Maybe I didn't always word my answers appropriately.
4. Request (for solution or repair)	I would really appreciate it if you could go over my paper and reconsider the marks you gave me.

If a positive outcome is expected, complaints should include some of the following elements:

- depersonalization of the problem,
- requests with modals such as *could/would*,
- use of mitigation (down-graders), and
- avoidance of blame and criticism.

Speaking Activity 6

Work in groups. Practise role-playing a complaint using the formula for making direct complaints. Perform your role-play for the class. The class will use the complaint evaluation checklist below to see if you have the formula correct and if the complaint sounds polite enough.

Complaint Evaluation Checklist

Complaint Formula	YES/NO	Comments
Were all parts of the complaint formula used?	_____	_____
Were modals of request used?	_____	_____
		_____
Does the complaint avoid criticism?	_____	_____
		_____
Was there a use of mitigation? (downplaying)	_____	_____
		_____
Was the complaint polite? Did it avoid placing blame?	_____	_____

Speaking Activity 7

Work with a partner. Organize these dialogues so that they are in the correct order. Then, choose one and practise saying it.

1. ☐ Miguel: Could you please, because I can't put up with this phone much longer.

   ☐ Miguel: Not really. Actually, could I just swap it for a less complicated model?

   ☐ Miguel: Well, it is very complicated and lights keep flashing all the time, and I really don't think it's straightforward enough for me to use. I keep getting my voicemail and text messages late, and I don't know how to adjust it to keep it working properly.

   ☐ Miguel: Hi, I wanted to talk to you about a cellphone I bought here last week.

   ☐ Salesperson: It depends on your contract, but I can check that for you.

   ☐ Salesperson: Sure. Anything wrong with it?

   ☐ Salesperson: I see. Do you want me to go over it with you?

2. ☐ Supervisor: I'm not sure I can. All the offices are occupied.

   ☐ Supervisor: OK, let me see what I can do.

   ☐ Supervisor: I see. Have you thought of keeping the door open?

   ☐ Supervisor: OK. Is there anything I can do about it?

   ☐ Maria: It doesn't seem to make any difference. Could you move me to an office that has better ventilation?

   ☐ Maria: It's very important that my clients and I have a space which doesn't give us headaches.

   ☐ Maria: I hope so, because the air is so stale that both the clients and I get terrible headaches after less than an hour in that room.

   ☐ Maria: I want to speak to you about the air in my office.

Speaking Activity 8

Work in groups of three. Talk about the last time you made a complaint. Compare your complaints with those of another group and report the most interesting complaints to the class.

Name	What Did You Complain About?	Who Did You Complain To?	What Did You Say?	What Was the Result?
_____	_____	_____	_____	_____
_____	_____	_____	_____	_____
_____	_____	_____	_____	_____
_____	_____	_____	_____	_____
_____	_____	_____	_____	_____

Speaking Activity 9

Work with a partner. In which of the following situations would you make a complaint? What result would you try to achieve? Choose a complaint and role-play it.

Situation	Would You Complain or Not?	Hoped-for Result?
You got a very low mark on an essay that took a long time to research and write.	_____	_____
You bought a pair of waterproof winter boots, but when you wore them you found that they leaked.	_____	_____
The pizza you ordered was delivered late and with completely different toppings than the ones you asked for.	_____	_____
In an expensive restaurant, the steak you ordered well-done arrived rare.	_____	_____
One of the students in your class was very rude to you and called you a rude name.	_____	_____
The neighbours above you have loud parties most Saturday nights.	_____	_____
A lot of people at school wear perfume or cologne, and you are allergic to it.	_____	_____
Your neighbours always cook very strong smelling foods, which you can smell in the hall.	_____	_____
You went to a movie during which the audience made so much noise that you missed half of the dialogue.	_____	_____
You received a lower mark in a speaking test than you expected, but everyone says your speaking is excellent.	_____	_____

Communication Focus: Indirect Complaints

In North American English, speakers use indirect complaints when they are speaking about a third party. The function of indirect complaints is to commiserate (complain about something/someone) and to establish a feeling of solidarity. Often indirect complaints are used to start conversations.

Indirect Complaint	**Response**
Yesterday's class was a total waste of time!	You can say that again. It was the worst!
I got a really low mark on my test. I don't think professor's questions were very clear.	I know. I couldn't understand them either, and that my mark was awful too.
The service in this restaurant is terrible. I don't how they have any customers.	Yeah. They're rude and sometimes they over- understand charge you. Yesterday, I had to ask them to correct my bill.

Speaking Activity 10

1. Work with a partner. Write possible responses to these indirect complaints. Then choose four and role-play them.

Complaints	**Responses**
This work is so boring. I can't stand it any more.	_____
The public transit in this city is really terrible. I can never get a bus when I need one.	_____
My boss is the most difficult person to get along with. Sometimes I feel like resigning.	_____
The weather this winter has been just terrible—one big snowstorm and cold front after another.	_____
My cellphone bills are so high that I'm going to go bankrupt if this continues. I wish there was a cheaper way.	_____
My neighbours are the messiest people! There's always something littering up their front yard.	_____

2. Work with a partner. Read the list of responses to indirect complaints. Decide what the complaint is, and write it down. Then practise saying the indirect complaints and responses.

Indirect Complaints	**Responses**
_____	I agree. It's driving me crazy too.
_____	Right on! I've never met anyone like that before either.
_____	Absolutely. My room is pretty bad too.
_____	You're right. It's horrible.
_____	I'm with you. She's the most disorganized person I know.
_____	You are so right. The food is really bad. I have to force myself to eat it.
_____	I know. I can't remember the last time we started on time.
_____	You're right. It was one of the worst.

Communication Focus: Comparing and Contrasting

When we want to compare two items in a short text, we can use the following expressions.

Expressions of Comparison	Examples
Both . . .	Both the USA and Canada are low context cultures.
Similarly . . .	Contracts are important in Canada. Similarly, contracts are very important in the USA.
Too/also/as well	Deadlines are important in Canadian business. They are important in business in Europe, too (also) (as well).
In the same way . . .	Meetings in Canada are organized. In the same way, meetings in Holland are also organized.
. . . is similar to . . . in that	Canada is similar to Denmark in that there are schedules and deadlines in business.
Like . . . ,	Like Americans, Canadians believe that contracts need to state everything involved in an agreement.

Expressions of Contrast	Examples
In contrast; however; on the other hand; differ from	The USA is a republic. In contrast, Canada is a monarchy.
	The USA is a republic. However, Canada is a monarchy.
	The USA is a republic. On the other hand, Canada is a monarchy.
	The USA is a republic. Canada differs from it in that it is a monarchy.
While; whereas	The USA is a republic, while Canada is a monarchy.
	The USA is a republic, whereas Canada is a monarchy.
Although; even though; in spite of	Although Canada is a monarchy, it is a democratic country.
	Even though Canada is a monarchy, it is a democratic country.
	In spite of being a monarchy, Canada is a democratic country.
. . . unlike . . .	Canada, unlike the USA, is a monarchy.

SPEAKING STRATEGY

If you give explanations or examples as you are speaking, others will find it easier to understand you. You can use "Let me explain" or "Here's an example" in order to give an explanation when speaking.

Speaking Activity 11

Work with a partner. Compare and contrast two countries that you are familiar with.

Factors	Country #1	Country #2
Size	_____	_____
Climate	_____	_____
People	_____	_____
Food	_____	_____
Other:	_____	_____
Other:	_____	_____
Other:	_____	_____

Speaking Activity 12

Work with a partner. One of you will read Section A and the other will read Section B. When you have finished, fill in the chart. Together make a five-minute presentation on some differences between high and low context cultures.

Section A: High Context Cultures

In a high context culture (which includes much of the Middle East, Africa, Asia, and South America), most people are from the same background. Everyone knows and understands all the rules, so there is no reason to state them explicitly. There are many things in the common context that help people understand the rules and so they can take a lot for granted. People in high context cultures emphasize the importance of relationships. In these cultures, there is a lot of reading between the lines, understanding metaphors, and understanding implicit messages. A lot depends on nonverbal communication. People's reactions are reserved and take place on the interior. There is strong loyalty to family and community. Developing trust is an important first step in any business relationship. High context cultures are collectivist, which means that the well-being of the group and harmony in the group are far more important than individual achievement. Relationships are more important than the tasks. People in these cultures place more importance on feelings and intuitions. Words are not as important as the context—which might be clear from the speaker's tone of voice, facial expression, gestures, posture, or even family background. Communication in high context cultures is often more indirect, more formal, and makes use of flowery language and elaborate speech acts. Writing agreements out in a contract is not usually appropriate and perhaps even insulting.

In high context cultures, there is a polychronic view of time. This means that human interaction is more valuable than time concerns and getting things done. Things eventually get done but in their own time. People often do many things at once. They are easily distracted. They put relationships first and focus on the goals rather than meeting deadlines. Being on time is less important than achieving goals.

Section B: Low Context Cultures

People in low context cultures come from a variety of different backgrounds because they are generally more mobile. They come and go, and so need to know the rules exactly and explicitly. Messages are explicit and clearly stated. There is no need to read between the lines. There is more focus on communicating with words than in nonverbal ways. People from low context cultures value reason, logic, directness, and simple language. Communication is straight forward. Statements need to use precise words which are taken literally. People believe they need contracts to spell out all the details of an agreement so that there will be no chance of getting confused. Contracts are detailed and explicit. The reactions of people in low context cultures are visible and outward.

People from low context cultures are individualistic and action-oriented. Solving a problem involves getting all the facts, analyzing them, and coming to a conclusion based on the facts. Decisions are based on facts rather than on feelings. Meetings and discussions end with actions that are based on the analysis of the problems. Groups are flexible, open, and changing as required by the circumstances. The bonds between people are not very strong and there is not a great sense of loyalty to the group. The task is always more important than the relationship.

The relationship to time in low context cultures is monochronic. This means doing one thing at a time, which requires organization, careful planning, and scheduling. In these cultures, people put the task first, emphasizing deadlines and getting the job done.

Factor	High Context Cultures	Low Context Cultures
Messages	Sometimes nonverbal, not openly stated	Explicit and clearly stated
Nonverbal communication		
Bonds between people		
Relationships		
People's reactions		
Contracts		
Relationship to time/deadlines		
Decisions		
Focus on group/individual		
Language		

Speaking Activity 13

There are a great many unusual laws in different parts of North America. Work with a partner. Decide whether the following laws are TRUE or FALSE. See the Answer Key to find the answers.

Law	TRUE/FALSE
In Washington State, you mustn't walk around in public if you are sick.	_____
Sleeping on a bench on a boardwalk in Delaware is illegal.	_____
It's illegal in Texas to eat your neighbour's garbage without his permission.	_____
In South Carolina, it's illegal for anyone under 18 to play pinball machines.	_____
In North Carolina, it is illegal to hold more than two sessions of bingo per week.	_____
In Illinois, a state law requires that a man's female companion call him "master" while out on a date. This does not apply to married couples.	_____
In Ottawa, it is illegal to have any kind of blue light on a non-authorized vehicle.	_____
In Nova Scotia, people mustn't water their lawns if it is raining.	_____
In Oshawa, it's illegal to climb trees.	_____
It's illegal in Canada to pay for a 26 cent item all in pennies (you can only use pennies up to 25 cents).	_____
Comic books mustn't show illegal acts in Canada.	_____
In Kanata, Ontario, it's illegal to have a clothesline in your backyard.	_____

Communication Focus: Expressing Warnings and Prohibitions

We use *had better* to express strong advice or warning. *Or else* is used to predict the consequences likely to occur if the warning is not listened to. We use *mustn't* to express prohibition. This means that something is not permitted by law or against the rules.

Structures/Expressions	Examples
. . . had better . . . . . . or else . . .	You had better go to the interview on time or else you won't get the job.
	You had better not stare at people or else they will think you are rude.
. . . mustn't . . .	You mustn't lie on your resumé.
	You mustn't borrow something without the owner's permission.

Other Structures to Express Prohibition

It's illegal to . . .	It's illegal to make and sell alcohol.
It's against the law to . . .	It's against the law to copy and sell books and movies.
. . . isn't allowed . . .	Copying and selling music isn't allowed in North America.

SPEAKING STRATEGY

If you ask questions during a conversation, this will help to keep the conversation going.

Examples

Excuse me, I have a question . . .
By the way . . .
Can you explain . . .
What do you mean . . .

 Please go to the website for more practice with this structure.

Speaking Activity 14

Work in groups of three. Imagine you are writing a guide book for tourists to three countries you know very well. Tell people what they *mustn't do* and what they *had better not do* in those countries. Predict the consequences of those actions. Report your ideas to the class.

Country	Prohibitions	Warnings	Consequences

Speaking Activity 15

Work in pairs and decide if the following actions are prohibited or not. Choose the correct modal. Check your answers with another pair and discuss the differences in laws in other countries. Report these differences to the class.

1. If you drink, you (mustn't, had better not, don't have to, shouldn't) drive.

2. If you want to serve alcohol at a large party in Ontario you (should, must, had better) get a liquor license.

3. If you want to drive a car, you (must, had better, should) have a driver's license.

4. If you are driving along the highway, you (mustn't, shouldn't, don't have to) throw paper out the window.

5. You (mustn't, shouldn't, had better not) be rude to police officers.

6. If you want to get married, you (must, had better, can) get a wedding license.

7. If you have an accident, you (mustn't, had better not, don't have to) drive away.

8. An employer in Canada (mustn't, doesn't have to, had better not) ask an employee's age or country of origin.

9. In Canada, people (mustn't, had better not, don't have to) hit anyone including spouses and children either at home or in public.

10. You (mustn't, shouldn't, had better not, don't have to) leave children under the age of 12 at home alone.

11. People (mustn't, shouldn't, had better not, don't have to) make any kind of sexual remarks or advances if the other person is not receptive.

Speaking Activity 16

Work with a partner. Interview each other and report the most interesting information or opinions to the class.

1. Do you believe in capital punishment? Why or why not?

2. Do you think we need stricter laws or punishment?

3. Do you think people should be able to freely copy books, movies, and music? Why or why not?

4. How do you feel about the police? Are you afraid of them/do you dislike them? Why?

5. Do you think governments have the right to ban certain habits such as smoking or using drugs?

6. Do you think there is more crime now than ten years ago?

7. Do you feel safe on the streets of your city?

8. Some people who have defended themselves during break-ins or robberies have been charged by the police. What do you think of this?

9. Do parents have the right to physically discipline their children? Why or why not?

10. Are there any crimes which you think should not be illegal? Please explain.

Listening 2

Before You Listen

Discuss these questions with your partner.

1. What are some laws which every country in the world recognizes?

2. What are some laws which exist only in some countries but not in others?

3. Have you ever broken the law? Please explain.

4. It is against the law to copy books, music, or movies without paying for them. What is your opinion on this issue?

5. Would you ever buy or trade products, such as watches, purses, clothes, which were pirated or copied without permission?

Pre-listening Vocabulary

You will hear these words and phrases in the interview you are going to listen to. Work with a partner or by yourself to write the correct vocabulary next to the definitions.

Vocabulary

creativity	theft	patronage	absurd
regulations	principles	digital	patent
statute	massive	controversial	shift
copyright	mish mash	morality	intellectual property
significance	holy grail	a pirate	information society
target	monopoly	livelihood	license
public domain	sanity	entertainment industry	knowledge economy

Definition

inventiveness, ingenuity, the ability to create new things

law

importance, meaningfulness

part of public cultural heritage, not protected by copyright, which the public has access to

fundamental rules, values, and philosophy

an assortment, collection of unrelated things, mixed up together

the exclusive ownership or control of something by one person or one company

financial support provided to artists and writers by patrons

stirring up debate, causing arguments

document giving official permission to do something

companies involved in providing entertainment, show business

the exclusive right granted by government to use or sell a creation

a person who robs others of their valuables or creations

creations of the mind—literary or artistic works

an economy based on creating and trading knowledge and ideas

a society in which creation, manipulation, and distribution of information is at the centre of daily life

move

ridiculous, crazy, illogical

a way of making a living, source of revenue, income

state of having ethics, principles, morals

describing the process of storing data, images, sounds, etc., using groups of electronic bits represented as 1 or 0

having a sound, healthy mind

very strongly desired object or outcome

huge, enormous, gigantic

robbery, stealing

aim, goal

the legal right granted to the creator of a work to produce, distribute, and sell his or her creation

rules or laws which govern actions

Vocabulary

Listening for the Main Ideas

Listen to the program on the audio CD once and answer these questions.

1. What are the two main points of view about copyright that are discussed in the program?

2. Why has the issue of copyright laws become so important?

3. Who owns ideas according to the narrator? Why?

 Listening Comprehension

Listen to the program again. Take notes to help you answer the following questions. As you listen, take notes about all the details that you hear under each heading. You can listen a second or third time to add more details to your notes. Check your notes with a partner.

1. What is the copy fight? What are the opposing sides?

_____

_____

2. What is Bill C-61? What is its goal?

_____

_____

3. What is file sharing?

_____

_____

4. What is the entertainment industry's opinion of file sharing?

_____

_____

5. Why does a growing number of people want stronger copyright laws?

_____

_____

6. What does copyright do?

_____

_____

7. The narrator says we are at a crisis or turning point. Why is this?

_____

8. What were the two main purposes of the first modern copyright laws?

_____

_____

 LISTENING STRATEGY

Mentally summarizing the main points a speaker makes will help you to understand the listening better.

 LISTENING STRATEGY

Taking notes focuses your attention and helps you follow the key ideas in a listening text.

9. Why did the US constitution permit lawmakers to pass copyright laws?

_____

_____

10. How has copyright changed today?

_____

_____

11. What does an information society need?

_____

_____

12. What is the narrator's opinion of the copyright issue?

_____

_____

Personalizing

Work in small groups. Discuss whether society should make and enforce stronger copyright laws or not. Try to reach consensus. Make a list of reasons to support your opinions.

Debate

The class can break up into two groups—those who support stronger copyright laws and those who think there should be free sharing of information and ideas. Make a list of your arguments and reasons, and then hold a debate on this.

Vocabulary and Language Chunks

Write the number of the expression next to the meaning. After checking your answers, choose six expressions and write your own sentences.

Expressions	**Meanings**
1. make the most of	☐ a scholar, a source of informed opinions
2. wrong way to go	☐ the point at which important changes or events occur
3. pundit	
4. turning point	☐ to make the best use of, to take advantage of
5. a necessary evil	☐ in a definite way, in a direct manner
6. land grab	☐ the use or enjoyment of something without spending money or effort
7. what's at the root of	
8. acute incidence	☐ not the correct method or procedure
9. the Internet age	☐ something we do not like but have to accept
10. free ride	☐ a fast acquisition of land or property by force
11. flat out	☐ what is the cause, source, origin of
12. a major shift	
13. controversial issue	☐ severe frequent occurrence
14. clog up	☐ a time in which information travels around the world in seconds, on the internet; information age
15. massive scale	
	☐ huge size, proportion
	☐ a problem which people have different opinions about, and which creates debates and controversy
	☐ an important change
	☐ block up, congest, choke

🎧 Pronunciation: Information Focus and Intonation

In conversations, the last content word in the sentence often receives the most emphasis. In this case, the rise or fall in intonation begins on the stressed syllable of this last content word. This is the word that is the most prominent (louder/longer/higher pitch), the word that the speaker thinks is the most important. This word is the information focus of the sentence. Listen to these examples on the audio CD.

What are you **doi**ng?	I'm taking a **break.**
You mustn't drive without a **lic**ense.	I got my license **yes**terday.
Is it rude to use this **ges**ture?	No, it's just **fine.**
Do you speak any other **lang**uages?	Yes, I speak **French.**

When the information focus is the last stressed content word in a sentence, this is called neutral focus.

Pronunciation Activity 1

Listen to these sentences on the audio CD and underline the focus words. Check your answers with a partner and the teacher. Then repeat these sentences to your partner in order to practise neutral focus.

Do a knuckle rap with your partner (touch your partner's knuckles with your own) as you say the focus word.

1. Copyright is a controversial issue.
2. They want us to make the most of the new tools for communication.
3. File sharing is the illegal copying of music and movies.
4. The entertainment industry believes that they are the victims of theft.
5. Copyright determines who owns and controls the expression of ideas.
6. Staring at people is considered impolite.
7. Etiquette and manners differ from country to country.
8. Is it rude to use a cellphone in church?
9. Do corporations want to own intellectual property?
10. Does Eric Flint's livelihood depend on royalties?
11. Do people buy and sell ideas to make money in an information society?
12. Will stronger copyright laws help build a knowledge economy?
13. Do you think that copyright laws are a necessary evil?

 Pronunciation Activity 2

As a conversation develops after the opening sentence, sometimes the focus changes to highlight new information. This depends on meaning and the context. In English, any word can receive focal stress. Listen to these dialogues. Then work with a partner to write two dialogues in which the focus of the information changes.

At school

Andrew: You look ex**haust**ed.
Bianca: I went to a **par**ty last night.
Andrew: What **kind** of party?
Bianca: A **birth**day party.

In a restaurant

Server: What'll you **have**?
Customer: A **ba**gel, a **toasted** bagel.
Server: Do you want any **cream** cheese?
Customer: No, **thanks**.
Server: Anything **else**?
Customer: **Coffee**, please.

Pronunciation Activity 3

Listen to these sentences on the audio CD, and circle the focus word. Check your answers.

1. What's the matter with you?
2. How about Friday morning?
3. It's more important than verbal language.
4. Do you believe in it?
5. Did he look the principal in the eye?
6. I don't feel safe anywhere.
7. Do you want me to look at the ceiling when people are speaking?
8. Men don't hold hands with each other.
9. How far should he stand?
10. Is there anything else to stare at?

Pronunciation Activity 4

Work with a partner. Circle what you think the focus word should be in the following sentences. Then decide which of the sentences in the previous exercise would make a good response to each sentence. Check your answers. Then practise these dialogues with your partner.

1. Andre: Could we possibly meet tomorrow morning?

   Beth: _____

2. Carlos: Do you believe in capital punishment?

   Rosa: _____

3. Laura: Is it alright for men to hold hands?

   Nelson: _____

4. Georgios: What's the matter?

   Anna: _____

5. Andrea: Don't stare at people in elevators.

   Brian: _____

6. Ellen: John stands too close to people.

   Lucy: _____

7. Abbas: It's not polite to look at the floor when someone is speaking.

   Summer: _____

8. Armando: He couldn't look the teacher in the eye.

   Edward: _____

9. Jonah: How important is non verbal language?

   Diego: _____

10. Eli: Do you feel safe in the city?

   Elizabeth: _____

Pronunciation Activity 5

Listen to these exchanges and underline the focus words in each sentence. How does this change the meaning? Check your answers and then practise these sentences with a partner.

1. Andrew: Copyright is a controversial issue.

   Libby: True, but is it the most controversial issue?

2. Serena: They want us to make the most of the new tools for communication.

   Jeff: Do they expect everyone to do that?

3. Alex: File sharing is the illegal copying of music and movies.

   Lisa: What do you call the legal copying of music and movies?

4. Judith: The entertainment industry believes that they are the victims of theft.

   Rosalie: But they don't know that they are the victims of theft.

5. Rashida: Copyright determines who owns and controls the expression of ideas.

   Henry: I don't know how anyone can own ideas.

 Pronunciation Activity 6

We use focus when we want to make contrasts. Listen to these examples.

1. I found some **useful** information and some **useless** information.
2. He'd like a glass of **red** wine and I'll have **white** wine.
3. My cousin lives in London, **Ontario**, not London, **England**.
4. He has a terrible **headache**, not a **stomach ache**.
5. He told me he had some **good** news and some **bad** news.

Work with a partner and underline the most prominent words in the following contrasts. Then listen to the sentences to check your answers. Practise saying these sentences with a partner and do a knuckle rap on the most prominent syllable of the contrasting words.

Example: I live in an a<u>**part**</u>ment not in a <u>**town**</u>house.

1. We live on the twelfth floor not the twentieth floor.
2. They spent hundreds of dollars, not thousands.
3. He believes in freeing the expression of ideas, not controlling it.
4. People are free to both express and experience creativity.
5. The public, and not the creators, should own ideas in an information society.
6. Both teachers and students need to be responsible.
7. It's against the law to steal and to cheat.
8. Robin went to London, Ontario, but I went to London, England.
9. Under the law in Canada, men and women are treated equally.
10. Both her brother and her sister are famous actors.
11. Both Canada and the USA are democracies.
12. Both Toronto and New York have stock markets.

Pronunciation Activity 7

Compare and contrast the USA and Canada. Work with a partner. One of you will complete Chart A and the other will complete Chart B. (Chart B is located in the Answer Key.) Exchange information to fill in your charts and make as many statements about Canada and the USA as you can.

Chart A

	Canada	USA
Head of government	Queen	President
Total area		
Size of population	Approximately 33,500,000	Approximately 307,500,000
GDP (gross domestic product) per capita	$44,823 US	$46,430 US
Disposable income per capita		
Life expectancy		
Nobel Prize winners		

 ## Pronunciation Activity 8

We use focus when we want to contradict or correct a statement. Listen to the following examples.

1. Her birthday is on January thirtieth.
   Really? I thought it was on January thirteenth.

2. Toronto is the capital of Canada.
   Are you sure? I think Ottawa is the capital.

3. The OK gesture is rude in the USA.
   I don't think so. I think it's fine in the USA.

4. Staring at people is polite in Canada and the US.
   Come on! It's rude to stare in Canada and the US.

The following are some incorrect statements. Work with a partner to correct them. Then practise saying them together using information focus stress to make the corrections.

Here are some other expressions to use in your corrections:

- Really?
- I think that . . .
- Are you sure?
- I thought that . . .
- I find that hard to believe
- Come on!

Example

Marta: Shanghai is the capital of China.

Bjorn: Are you sure? I think that Beijing is the capital of China.

1. *Romeo and Juliet* was written by Hemingway.
2. Maintaining eye contact during conversation isn't important in the US and Canada.
3. San Francisco is the biggest city in the USA.
4. All writers and film makers want strong copyright laws.
5. Relationships and loyalty to family and community are features of low context cultures.
6. The USA and Canada are high context cultures.
7. Contracts are necessary in high context cultures.
8. The expression "time is money" shows the importance of time in polychromic cultures.
9. In Canada, it's legal to copy movies and sell them to your friends.
10. The USA is as big as Canada.
11. People in Canada have more disposable income than people in the USA.

Communicating in the Real World

Try to use your English to talk to people outside your class. Work with a partner to make up a questionnaire asking four to eight questions about one of the following topics. Show your questions to the teacher. Then speak to people who are not in your class and report to the class what you learned.

Topics: Body language and gestures; cultural differences (eye contact, space, touching, etc.); dating and marriage; laws; high context and low context cultures; and copyright in music, books, and movies.

Self Evaluation

Rate yourself (using a scale of 0–5, where "5" is the highest ranking) and write your comments in each section of the chart. Show the chart to your teacher and discuss your strengths and weaknesses.

Topic	Good (5, 4)	Improving (3, 2)	Needs more work (1, 0)
Grammar and Language Functions 1. Making recommendations and predicting consequences 2. Making direct and indirect complaints 3. Comparing and contrasting 4. Expressing warnings and prohibitions			
Speaking Strategies 1. Paraphrasing or restating helps you to make sure that others understand you. 2. If you add information and ideas during a conversation, this will help to keep the conversation going. 3. If you give explanations or examples as you are speaking, others will find it easier to understand you. 4. What other speaking strategies did you use?			
Listening Strategies 1. Try to guess the meaning of phrases you do not understand by using your knowledge of the context and your background knowledge. 2. Taking notes focuses your attention and helps you follow the key ideas in a listening text. 3. What other listening strategies did you use?			
Pronunciation Focus words and intonation			

Vocabulary and Language Chunks

Write 10 sentences using vocabulary from the chapter.

1. _____
2. _____
3. _____
4. _____
5. _____
6. _____
7. _____
8. _____
9. _____
10. _____

My plan for practising is . . . _____

_____

_____

CHAPTER 8
Nature and the Environment

Read the following quote. Do you agree? Explain why or why not.

> "Our ancestors viewed the Earth as rich and bountiful, which it is. Many
> people in the past also saw nature as inexhaustibly sustainable, which
> we now know is the case only if we care for it. It is not difficult to forgive
> destruction in the past which resulted from ignorance. Today, however, we
> have access to more information, and it is essential that we re-examine
> ethically what we have inherited, what we are responsible for, and what we
> will pass on to coming generations. . . . The exploration of space takes place
> at the same time as the Earth's own oceans, seas, and fresh water areas
> grow increasingly polluted. Many of the Earth's habitats, animals, plants,
> insects . . . may not be known at all by future generations. We have the
> capability, and the responsibility. We must act before it is too late."
>
> — His Holiness Tenzin Gyatso, the Fourteenth Dalai Lama of Tibet,
> spiritual leader of the Buddhist faith

Communication Focus: Taking Turns in Conversation

In conversation, we use certain expressions, questions, and body language to
let people know that we are ready to give up the floor and let someone else
speak. When someone is ready to give up the floor, he or she will usually pause
and use one of these expressions.

Expressions

That's about all I have to say. What do you think?

What's your reaction/opinion/point of view/your thoughts?

How do you feel?

That's my opinion. What about you?

Speakers who want to keep speaking use the following strategies:

1. They don't pause at the end of their sentences. They place their pauses at
   points where the message is clearly incomplete.

2. They make their sentences run on by using connectors like *and, then, but,
   so*, etc.

Body Language

A speaker who is ready to give up the floor can pick a specific person to continue the conversation by turning towards the person, looking at him or her and/or by asking questions. Looking down or away can signal that anyone can continue the conversation.

Expressions to Signal that You Want the Floor

Well, I'd like to say . . .   Well, if you ask me . . .   Well in my opinion . . .

Speaking Activity 1

Work in groups of three. Rank the animals in each category below from 1 to 10, with "1" being the most beautiful, "2" being the second most beautiful, etc. Use expressions for stating opinions and taking turns in conversation. When you finish, each group will present their results so that everyone can compare their answers.

SPEAKING STRATEGY

When you are speaking, take a chance and try to express your ideas if you have something that you want to say. Don't worry about sounding foolish or making mistakes. The most important thing is to get your idea across.

The Most Beautiful	The Most Interesting	The Most Intelligent	The Most Dangerous
tiger	tiger	tiger	tiger
dolphin	dolphin	dolphin	dolphin
wolf	wolf	wolf	wolf
zebra	zebra	zebra	zebra
elephant	elephant	elephant	elephant
monkey	monkey	monkey	monkey
shark	shark	shark	shark
panda bear	panda bear	panda bear	panda bear
lion	lion	lion	lion
whale	whale	whale	whale

Communication Focus: Using the Passive Voice to Ask For and Give Impersonal Information

When we give impersonal information, we often use the passive voice. This focuses attention on the object or the person that received the action, not the person who performed the action.

Examples

Active Voice: The WWF (World Wildlife Fund) **raises** money to protect animals.
Passive Voice: Money to protect animals **is raised** by the WWF.

Active: WWF-Canada (World Wildlife Fund) protects 96 million acres of Canadian wilderness.
Passive: 96 million acres of Canadian wilderness are protected by WWF-Canada.

Active: Senator Alan MacNaughton founded WWF-Canada in 1967.
Passive: WWF-Canada was founded in 1967 by Senator Alan MacNaughton.

Please go to the website for more practice with this structure.

Speaking Activity 2

Here's a list of statements from a press release about WWF-Canada. Work with a partner and change all the active sentences to the passive voice. Then, choose the five that you think are the most important facts. Present your list of the five most important facts about WWF-Canada to the class.

Facts about WWF-Canada

1. WWF-Canada supports research to protect Canadian wildlife and habitats.

2. They are setting up a network of protected marine areas.

3. They have tackled conservation challenges facing Canada.

4. They have developed recovery plans for whales in the St Lawrence River.

5. WWF-Canada supports groups who want to save the natural world.

Past Successes

1. WWF-Canada has saved thousands of acres of tropical rain forests in South America.

2. They protected over 10 million hectares of wilderness in the Mackenzie River delta from industrial development.

3. With the help of a corporate sponsor, they took the white pelican off the endangered list.

4. They moved shipping lanes in the Bay of Fundy away from whale feeding grounds.

Speaking Activity 3

Work with a partner and decide if these statements are TRUE or FALSE. State your opinions even if you are not sure. Share your opinions with the rest of the class.

1. Elephants are the largest land animal.

2. Elephants die at about age 40 in captivity and in their 70s in the wild.

3. Elephants live in groups of females such as mothers, aunts, grandmothers, juveniles, and infants.

4. An adult elephant needs to walk around 50 kilometres per day in order to stay healthy.

5. Most zoos can't care for elephants properly because they don't give them enough space.

6. Elephants need approximately 100 acres of wide open space.

7. Male elephants are rarely seen in zoos because they are bigger, more aggressive, and need larger enclosures than the females.

8. Animal rights advocates are calling on all zoos to close down elephant exhibits and send the elephants to sanctuaries.

Please see the Answer Key to find out the answers.

Listening 1

Before You Listen

Pre-listening Vocabulary

You will hear these words and phrases in the interview. Work with a partner or by yourself to write the correct vocabulary next to the definitions.

Vocabulary

miniscule	protocols	misguided	to breed	illicit
animal rights	captivity	fragmentation	a sham	drive
organization	corral	marginally	welfare	to be vocal
to be banned	facility	habitat	roam	ivory trade
calf	to boost	strategy	horrendous	

Definition	Vocabulary
extremely small	_____
a baby elephant	_____
to be forbidden, prohibited	_____
set of rules and procedures	_____
a pen or enclosure for large animals such as horses	_____
to make better, improve	_____
a group of people who advocate on behalf of animals	_____
confinement, internment, prevented from being free	_____
a building or structure designed and built for a specific purpose	_____
mistaken, erroneous	_____
slightly, a tiny bit	_____
to break into pieces or fragments, disintegration, destruction	_____
home, environment	_____
tactic, plan	_____
a deception, pretense, fraud	_____
to cause to reproduce	_____
to travel, wander	_____
health and well being	_____
illegal, unlawful, criminal	_____
awful, terrible, dreadful	_____
to speak up loudly and frequently	_____
strong force, impetus	_____
trade in the bones of elephants	_____

Listening for the Main Ideas

Listen to the interview once and answer these questions.

1. What changes have occurred at the Calgary Zoo recently?

2. What is Rob Laidlaw's general opinion of elephants in zoos?

3. What are the two opposing ideas discussed in this interview?

 Listening Comprehension

Listen to the interview again. In the notes below, the main topics discussed in the interview are listed on the left. Some of the details about each topic are on the right. As you listen, check the details and add to the notes. You may want to listen several times. Check your notes with a partner and your teacher.

Topics	Details
Significant event at Calgary Zoo	new baby elephant was born at the zoo
Animal rights organizations	speak on behalf of animals, especially elephants
Reactions by Rob Laidlaw, executive director of Zoo Check Canada	this is not a victory for conservation
Calgary Zoo's "Elephant crossing"	newly opened home for elephants at the zoo
Rob Laidlaw's opinion of "Elephant crossing"	the cost was very high
Rob Laidlaw's opinion of the breeding of animals in zoos	breeding is not a sign of welfare
Calgary Zoo's plans to handle the new situation according to spokesman Kevin Strange	Calgary Zoo reviewed its practices or protocols
Calgary Zoo's conservation, outreach, and research program	Calgary Zoo has a significant conservation, outreach, and research program

Topics	Details
Rob Laidlaw's opinion of the benefits of the work of zoos in conservation and education	the trickle-down theory of money for conservation is a theory that zoos like to talk about _____ _____
Rob Laidlaw's reactions to claims made by zoos about the dangers elephants face in the wild	not true that elephants are shot in the wild everywhere _____ _____ _____
Zoo Check's requirements for animals in captivity	if we have animals in captivity we need to examine their biological and behavioural needs _____

Personalizing

Work in small groups of three or four. Decide which of the two opposing views about elephants or other animals in zoos your group supports. Give reasons for your decision.

Vocabulary and Language Chunks

Write the number of the expression next to the meaning. After checking your answers, choose six expressions and write your own sentences.

Expressions

1. the bottom line
2. in a perfect world
3. at face value
4. to buy into
5. in the wild
6. not to hold water
7. trickle down theory
8. you can bet
9. the low end of the scale
10. a cause for celebration
11. stress free
12. off site
13. quality of life
14. dire circumstances

Meanings

☐ the argument put forward is not logical, reasonable, or strong; it doesn't make sense

☐ growing or living in a natural state

☐ in the lowest category

☐ ability to enjoy normal life activities, and to live a satisfying life

☐ in a different spot or location

☐ extremely poor situation

☐ the way things look on the surface, superficial appearance

☐ without tension, worries, or difficulties

☐ to agree with, accept as true and valid

☐ the idea that growth and money in the largest institutions will eventually benefit the entire system; the theory that benefits will eventually reach the lowest level

☐ you can be sure, certain about

☐ a reason to rejoice, be happy, and have a party

☐ the most important factor, thing, consideration

☐ ideally, in the best of all possible circumstances

Communication Focus: Expressing Disapproval

Structures/Expressions	Examples
It's terrible/horrible/dreadful/awful that . . .	It's dreadful that factories are allowed to pollute lakes.
I disapprove of . . .	I disapprove of allowing factories to discharge chemicals into lakes.
I am really against . . .	I am really against factories discharging their waste into lakes.
It's unacceptable that . . .	It's unacceptable that factories are able to discharge waste into lakes.

Less Direct Disapproval Statements

I don't understand why . . .	I don't understand why factories are allowed to discharge waste into lakes.
I don't like . . .	I don't like factories discharging waste into lakes.
I don't think . . .	I don't think factories should be able to discharge waste into lakes and streams.
Questions	Why are factories allowed to discharge waste into lakes?

Speaking Activity 4

On their website, the group People for the Ethical Treatment of Animals (PETA) makes the following statements. Work with a partner and make a list of eight things people do to animals which PETA disapproves of. What do you and your partner disapprove of the most?

1. Animals Are Not Ours to Eat.

2. Animals Are Not Ours to Wear.

3. Animals Are Not Ours to Experiment On.

4. Animals Are Not Ours to Use for Entertainment.

5. Animals Are Not Ours to Abuse in Any Way.

Speaking Activity 5

Work with a partner. Rank the environmental dangers from the most serious ("1") to the least serious ("10"). Then join another pair and compare your answers. Report the five actions that your group disapproves of the most.

☐ Burning fossil fuels (petroleum, coal) to produce energy is widespread.

☐ Putting garbage into landfill sites is done everywhere.

☐ Burying nuclear waste in the earth and dumping it into oceans is a common practice.

☐ Population growth: the world's population is approximately 7 billion people and will be 9 billion by 2040.

☐ More and more plants and animals are becoming extinct.

☐ Emission of greenhouse gases has caused the temperature to increase worldwide.

- [ ] Rivers, lakes, and oceans are becoming more polluted.

- [ ] Overfishing has greatly reduced the number of fish in the oceans.

- [ ] The use of cars has dramatically increased all over the globe.

- [ ] More people are living in cities than ever before.

- [ ] Oil spills have caused, and are still causing, great damage to oceans and coastal areas, and to the birds, fish, and animals which inhabit them.

Communication Focus: Criticizing

This is a very strong way to express disapproval. It is used in making an argument or stating strong disapproval. In casual or friendly conversation, people use more diplomatic, very indirect ways of criticizing.

Structure/Expressions	Examples
. . . to be wrong	Keeping animals in zoos is wrong.
. . . to be terrible/awful/horrible	Wearing fur coats is horrible.
. . . shouldn't . . .	Hunters shouldn't kill baby seals.
. . . should . . .	Canada should ban seal hunting.
. . . shouldn't have + *past participle*	The oil spill shouldn't have happened.
. . . should have + *past participle*	The company should have been forced to clean up the oil.
. . . to be supposed to . . .	The government is supposed to protect the environment.
	Hunters aren't supposed to kill endangered species of animals.

Grammar Note

One of the language functions that *to be supposed to* . . . fulfills is criticizing. Please note the various forms and meanings.

Form	Meaning	Example
To be supposed to + base form of verb	It is expected.	You threw the bottle in the garbage, but you are supposed to put it into the recycling bin.
Not to be supposed to + base form of verb	It isn't allowed.	You are not supposed to smoke near this building.
Was/were supposed to + base form of the verb	It was expected to happen but did not.	They were supposed to close the elephant exhibit last year, but it's still open.
Wasn't/weren't supposed to + base form of the verb	It wasn't allowed but the action was carried out.	They weren't supposed to fish in these waters, but they did it any way.

 Please go to the website for more practice with this structure.

Speaking Activity 6

Work in groups of three. Read the passage below. Discuss the actions and decide which three actions your group criticizes the most. List them in order, with "1" being the worst, "2" being the second worst, etc. Then research three species that are endangered and the reasons for this. Discuss ways in which these species could be saved. Report to the class.

Disappearing Species

Scientists say the earth supports between five million and 80 million species but only a million and a half have been found and classified so far. However, entire species are disappearing or are about to disappear before we have a chance to learn how they benefit the environment and what part they play in biodiversity.

Can you imagine a meadow without flowers or a lake without fish? According to Swiss scientists this is going to happen. They estimate that approximately 100 species become extinct each day worldwide. The earth's biodiversity is in serious danger. Some experts are even saying that the number of species will be cut in half by 2050. One in four mammals, one in eight birds, one third of all amphibians and 70 per cent of the world's catalogued plants now appear on the list of endangered species. According to the World Conservation Union, the extinction rate is 10,000 times higher than expected. Human activity and climate change are the biggest threats to plants and animals.

In Brazil and other countries, thousands of hectares of rainforest are destroyed each year. Each year in North America, more and more farmland is used to build housing. As a result, many birds, animals, and plants are losing their natural habitats. Some birds such as whooping cranes and spotted owls have almost disappeared from North America. Gorillas, tigers, whales, and sharks are some of the better known victims on the endangered species list. In the Arctic Ocean, icebergs and glaciers are melting due to global warming. When the ice disappears, polar bears and seals which inhabit the ice will be unable to survive. At one time, not so long ago, large parts of North America, Europe, and Asia were covered with thick forests. Mankind has put an end to most of these. A great many plants, possibly holding the secrets to curing deadly diseases, have also disappeared with the forests. When a plant or animal species becomes extinct, all the other species that depend on it are affected because all of life is interconnected. As a species, we humans need to realize that we are a part of nature and that what happens to the environment affects us physically, culturally, and emotionally.

Worst Actions

1. _____

2. _____

3. _____

Endangered Species	**Reasons**	**Solutions**
_____	_____	_____
_____	_____	_____
_____	_____	_____
_____	_____	_____
_____	_____	_____

Communication Focus: Eliciting and Analyzing Opinions
Expressing Various Degrees of Certainty

Structures/Expressions for Eliciting Opinions

What do you think of . . . ?
What's your opinion of (about) . . . ?
How do you feel about . . . ?

Structures/Expressions for Analyzing Opinions

Do you really think/ feel believe . . .
Do you really mean to say . . . ?
Can you really say that . . . ?

Structures/Expressions for Various Degrees of Certainty

Less Certain/ Diplomatic	Neutral	Very Certain
It seems to me . . .	I think/feel/believe . . .	I'm certain/sure/positive . . .
I imagine . . .	I'd like to say . . . /point out . . .	I honestly feel/believe/ think . . .
To the best of my knowledge . . .	The point is . . .	I'm convinced that . . .
As far as I know . . .	Not everyone will agree with me but . . .	In my (honest) opinion . . .
People say . . .	I'm pretty sure/certain . . .	There's no question in my mind . . .
I've heard that . . .	If you ask me . . .	
Don't you think that . . . /Wouldn't you say that . . .		

Responses

Less Certain/Neutral	Strong Agreement	Strong Disagreement
I suppose so/not.	Absolutely!	Absolutely not!
I guess you're right.	You're absolutely right!	I totally disagree.
If you think so.	No question about it!	I'm convinced that's not true/right.
It's worth some thought.	I totally agree.	How can you say that?
I'm not sure I agree.	I couldn't agree more.	Are you kidding?
Not everyone would agree.	I'm convinced/sure you're right!	No way!
Really?	Right on!	

Speaking Activity 7

Work in groups of four. Find out how everyone feels about the following issues. Use expressions that show how strongly you feel. Report to the class.

1. In your opinion, what are some of the worst things people have done to wild animals?

2. Do you think pets should be treated like people? For example, North Americans spend over 40 billion dollars on their pets each year. What's your opinion of this?

3. Do you believe animals can communicate? Explain why.

4. What do you think animals might say about humans if they could communicate?

5. Do you think animals should have rights? Please explain.

6. What can human beings learn from animals?

7. Do you think some animals can think and can express their feelings? Please explain.

8. What in your opinion are some differences between people and animals? Please explain.

9. What different views of animals are there in other countries and cultures? For example, in North America a dog is considered man's best friend, whereas in some countries dogs are thought to be very low, dirty animals.

10. Which of the following do you believe exist? Please explain.
    a) Vampires
    b) Werewolves
    c) Mermaids
    d) The Loch Ness Monster
    e) Bigfoot (also known as Sasquatch, a huge apelike creature which is said to inhabit mountain forests)
    f) Other unusual creatures

Speaking Activity 8

In English, there are many expressions comparing people to animals in different ways. Work with a partner to complete these expressions and write sentences using them. Check your answers with another pair of students. Then make up a dialogue using some of these expressions.

Example

As busy as a bee—Ellen was as busy as a bee making plans for her dinner party.

1. as sick as _____
2. as hungry as _____
3. as playful as _____
4. as slow as _____
5. as quiet as _____

6. as stubborn as _____
7. as big as _____
8. as free as _____
9. as clever as _____
10. as proud as _____

Speaking Activity 9

Work in groups of three. Discuss what the animal idioms and expressions in the sentences mean. Use expressions for stating opinions and taking turns in conversation. When you have finished, check your answers with the teacher, and then make up a dialogue using some of these idioms.

1. Henry's bark is worse than his bite.
   a) He barks like a dog when he is angry.
   b) He makes a lot of noise but nothing comes of it.
   c) He doesn't have any teeth.
   d) He likes to play with dogs.

2. It's a dog-eat-dog world in business and Andrea hates it.
   a) Andrea hates eating dog meat.
   b) Andrea hates dogs because they bite each other.
   c) Andrea doesn't like the competition in business.
   d) Andrea hates business.

3. Eleanor drinks like a fish.
   a) She drinks a lot of water.
   b) She drinks very quickly.
   c) She doesn't like to drink a lot.
   d) She drinks a lot of alcohol.

4. Miriam is a very catty person.
   a) She looks like a cat.
   b) She loves cats.
   c) She sounds like a cat when she speaks.
   d) She talks about other people behind their backs.

5. Abby never socializes so she felt like a fish out of water at the party.
   a) She felt uncomfortable and strange at the party.
   b) She talked to a lot of people at the party.
   c) She enjoyed herself.
   d) She was not very active at the party.

6. Mei-Ling eats like a bird.
   a) She doesn't chew her food very well.
   b) She eats very frequently.
   c) She likes to eats seeds and grains.
   d) She doesn't eat very much.

7. Daniel is very pig-headed.
   a) He has a fat, round face.
   b) He has a very short, stout nose.
   c) His head is very round and bald.
   d) He is a very stubborn person.

8. Alex is always horsing around.
   a) His favourite pastime is riding horses.
   b) He is a very loud person.
   c) He takes very large steps when he walks.
   d) He likes to joke around and play tricks on people.

9. Karen let the cat out of the bag.
   a) She let the cat run away.
   b) She told a secret.
   c) She spent a lot of money.
   d) She got very angry at someone.

10. People talked about everything and ignored the elephant in the room, Michelle's illness.
    a) They didn't want to talk about animals.
    b) They are afraid of elephants.
    c) They didn't want to talk about Michelle's illness.
    d) They ignored Michelle.

11. What Vladimir makes from his part-time job is chicken feed.
    a) He works to buy food for his chickens.
    b) He makes very little money.
    c) He has to get up early for his part-time job.
    d) His job is not very interesting.

12. Lucy thinks that studying is for the birds.
    a) She believes it's very important.
    b) She doesn't feel it's very important.
    c) She studies only a little every day.
    d) Studying is very easy for her.

13. Missing the deadline was the straw that broke the camel's back and George was fired.
    a) He was fired because, in addition to many other mistakes, he missed the deadline.
    b) George was fired because he hurt a camel.
    c) George was fired because he missed the deadline.
    d) George was fired because he made a lot of mistakes.

14. Mark is squirreling away his money.
    a) He is saving his money.
    b) He is spending his money slowly.
    c) He is investing his money.
    d) He is giving away his money to his friends.

15. The clients want to buy that house and are ready to talk turkey.
    a) They are ready to talk about all the problems.
    b) They are ready to buy the house after Christmas.
    c) They want to talk frankly and to make an offer.
    d) They want to fool the owners of the house.

Speaking Activity 10

Here is a TRUE/FALSE quiz about the human animal and the differences
between the sexes. Complete the quiz with a partner. State your opinions.
Compare your answers with the answers in the Answer Key, which are based on
research findings. What surprised you the most?

Statement	TRUE	FALSE
1. Women have a greater capacity for feeling happy than men do.	_____	_____
2. Women are better at learning and using language than men are.	_____	_____
3. Men are more accurate at throwing or catching objects than women.	_____	_____
4. Women are more talkative and communicative than men.	_____	_____
5. Women have more trouble reading maps than men.	_____	_____
6. Men are better at mathematics than women.	_____	_____
7. Men and women have different approaches to problem solving.	_____	_____
8. Men and women have different kinds of dreams.	_____	_____
9. Men lie more often than women.	_____	_____
10. In stressful situations, men and women respond very differently.	_____	_____

Communication Focus: Persuading/Countering Arguments

After you express an opinion or make a suggestion, people may not agree. They
may argue a different point of view and try to persuade you to see their side.

Structures/Expressions	Examples
I see your point but . . .	A: Driving a car is the most air polluting act that the average citizen performs. B: I see your point, but in the modern world how else can people get where they need to go?
That's probably true, but . . . That may be so, but . . . Possibly, but . . .	A: Cars contribute to greenhouse gas accumulation in the atmosphere and are responsible for climate changes. B: That's probably true, but we rely on cars to get around. What would we do without them?

Wouldn't you agree that . . .	A: Wouldn't you agree that local and global pollution would be reduced if each person drove 30–40 per cent less?
On the other hand . . .	B: On the other hand, if people drove less, the car industry and the gasoline industry would suffer.
Look at it this way . . .	B: Look at it this way, if cities improved public transportation, people wouldn't use cars so much.
No question about it.	A: If car drivers had to pay for the miles they drove, and if the cost increased as the miles driven increased, they would drive much less. No question about it!
You can't go wrong . . .	A: You can't go wrong limiting car use. People will be healthier. City air will be cleaner. There will be less environmental damage.

Speaking Activity 11

Work with a partner. Discuss the arguments for and against driving. Decide which ones you agree with. Then one of you will choose the arguments for driving and the other will counter the arguments. After you finish, the class can divide into two groups and have a debate on this statement: **Cars do more damage than good.**

Arguments for Driving	**Arguments against Driving**
Cars give people mobility and freedom. Without cars, there would be many isolated communities.	Passengers have a higher mortality rate in cars than on trains, buses, and commercial aircraft.
Riding bicycles is tiring and uncomfortable and not very good for older people or people with disabilities.	Cars burn a mixture of compounds which generate CO_2. These emissions contribute to global warming.
Cars do not cause accidents. Drivers do. Driver education needs to be upgraded and improved. Regulations need to be enforced.	As more people drive cars, the environment loses green spaces to highways and parking lots, which are not only ugly, but result in higher temperatures, affecting a city's microclimate.
Electric cars, cars running on ethanol, and hybrid cars are being developed to solve the pollution and energy problems.	Car use should be a privilege, not a right. The cost of environmental damage has to be added to the cost of owning and operating a car. Vehicle use should no longer be subsidized by the general public.
Driving a car can open up opportunities for jobs and homes in farther off places. People do not need to be tied to particular locations.	Cities have become islands of toxic chemicals because drivers are completely free to use vehicles burning fossil fuels. Cars are noisy, ugly, often dangerous, and dominate the experience of modern living.

People who own and drive cars have a more pleasant, less stressful, more convenient existence.

Car ownership results in more jobs in sales and service and builds up the economy.

Public transportation is often crowded, unreliable, and inconvenient. It takes much longer to get anywhere by public transportation.

Driving saves time and increases a person's productivity.

Driving puts a person in control of his or her plans, and gives people more choices and opportunities, and in these ways makes them happier and more confident.

Car fumes contain known cancer-causing chemicals such as benzene.

The cost of cars and gasoline does not pay the high indirect costs of driving such as the waste of land and energy, the expenses of traffic enforcement, pollution, and the cost of accidents by uninsured drivers.

When all the solutions to the damage caused by cars are considered, no solution is better than having fewer vehicles and restricting the use of vehicles.

Traffic accidents kill and injure people, but they also leave many suffering from disabilities and psychological damage.

Crowded roads and traffic congestion lead to stress in drivers and incidents of road rage.

Speaking Activity 12

Work with a partner. Read the following suggestions as to what governments should do about cars. Decide which ones you both agree with and produce counter arguments for those you disagree with.

In order to reduce the use of cars and vehicles governments should…

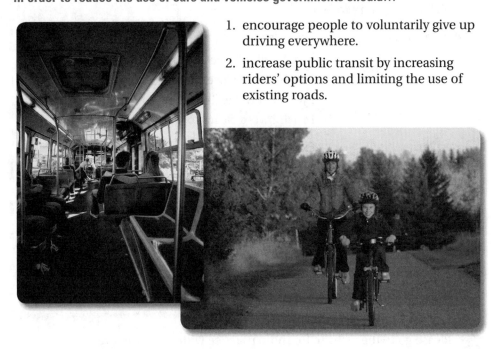

1. encourage people to voluntarily give up driving everywhere.
2. increase public transit by increasing riders' options and limiting the use of existing roads.

3. separate commercial and private traffic to increase efficient use of roads.

4. stop building roads and highways.

5. replace 30–40 per cent of the existing roads designed for cars with parks.

6. build more walking paths, bicycle routes, and roads for small electric vehicles in cities.

7. reward car-pools and car-sharing.

8. regulate road use by giving access privileges to cars with more passengers.

9. charge road tolls and increase gasoline and vehicle registration taxes.

10. tie car license fees to fuel consumption in the previous year so that individuals who used a lot of gasoline the previous year will pay higher fees.

11. provide generous development grants and tax incentives for all non-polluting transportation alternatives.

Communication Focus: Expressing Regrets

Expressions/Structures	Examples
It's too bad . . .	It's too bad that cars pollute the environment so much.
I (really) regret . . .	I really regret buying a car.
I'm sorry that (about) . . .	I'm sorry that everyone wants to drive a car.
I wish . . .	I wish people could get along without cars.

Grammar Note

When we use *wish* to express regrets, we are talking about situations which are contrary to fact.

Present Tense	Examples
. . . wish + past form	I wish I didn't need to drive to work (but I do).
	I wish I lived closer to work (but I don't).
	I wish I could walk to work (but I can't).
	I wish I were closer to work (but I am not).

Past Tense	Examples
. . . wish + past perfect	Monica wishes she hadn't had to drive to school last year (but she did).
	She wishes she had been able to get along without a car (but she wasn't).

Future tense	Examples
. . . wish + would	I wish people would stop producing so much garbage (but I don't think they will).

Please go to the website for more practice with this structure.

Speaking Activity 13

Work with a partner. What are six things you wish/regret about the following facts? Compare your answers with another pair of students and report the most interesting ideas to the class.

1. The world population is approaching seven billion people.
2. Global warming is melting the ice in the Arctic and Antarctic regions.
3. The ozone in the atmosphere is being depleted and this will lead to an increase in ultraviolet radiation which causes cancer.
4. Heavy demands on the world's surface waters have resulted in serious shortages. Pollution of rivers, lakes, and ground water further limits the supply.
5. There is a shortage of fish due to overfishing, and large areas of the ocean are so polluted that they are now dead zones.
6. Tropical rain forests, as well as temperate forests, are being destroyed rapidly. Some forest types will be gone in a few years and most by the end of the century.
7. The loss of species is very serious. We are losing the possibilities they hold for medicinal and other benefits, and the contribution that they make to the world's biological systems and to the incredible beauty of the earth.
8. Worldwide demand for gasoline leads oil companies to drill for oil without taking all the necessary precautions, and this can result in horrible damages from oil spills.
9. Other issue/concern

Speaking Activity 14

Work with a partner. What are some personal regrets you have about yourself?

Regrets	Me	My Partner
In what ways do you wish you were different?	_____	_____
Where do you wish you lived?	_____	_____
What do you wish you did for a living?	_____	_____
How many languages do you wish you spoke?	_____	_____
What do you wish you could do?	_____	_____
How much money do you wish you had?	_____	_____
What do you wish you didn't have to do?	_____	_____
What is a regret you have about something you did in the past?	_____	_____
What is a regret you have about something you didn't do in the past?	_____	_____

Communication Focus: Reporting Information

Direct Speech

This occurs when we report what the speaker said by using the speaker's words. Research shows that direct speech is rarely the exact quotation but often a re-wording or summary of what the speaker said. There is no change of tenses in direct speech. The verb *say* is used most frequently.

Examples

John called and said, "I'm ready to start work," but his boss said, "I'm sorry, your job has been eliminated."

In very informal conversation among young adults, people also use *go, be like,* and *be all* to report direct quotes.

Examples

He gets mad and goes, "I don't like to eat leftovers."

So she goes, "Then, why don't you learn to cook or something."

And I'm like, "Listen, I'm not complaining."

So he's all, "Sorry about that. Please let me take you out."

Indirect Speech

When we report information, not using the direct words of the speaker, we use verbs such as *say, tell, state, ask, answer, respond, inquire, reply,* and *argue.*

Examples

The expert said that global warming was melting the ice in the Arctic.

The newspaper reported that the conference would study ways of saving endangered species.

Note: *Say* and *tell* are different. Use *say* when reporting what *was said*; use *tell* when reporting *who said something to whom.*

Examples

The newspapers said that the global climate was changing.

The president told the people that he would wage war on climate change.

Grammar Note

In reported speech, when the first verb is in the past tense, the tenses of the following verbs change in the following ways:

Present . . . changes to . . . Past

"The glaciers are melting faster."	He said that the glaciers **were melting** faster.
"Global warming causes more droughts."	He said that global warming **caused** more droughts.

Past and Present Perfect . . . change to . . . Past Perfect

"Many people drowned during the flood."	The reporter stated that many people had drowned during the flood.
"The tsunami has killed several thousand people."	The announcer reported that the tsunami **had killed** several thousand people.

Will/Can/May . . . change to . . . Would/Could/Might

"Demands for fresh water will grow as the earth becomes warmer."	They reported that demands for fresh water **would grow** as the earth became warmer.
"Severe pollution can kill all living things in the lake."	The expert stated that severe pollution **could kill** all living things in the lake.
"Ocean creatures which we have not yet studied may hold the key to curing certain illnesses."	The marine biologist argued that ocean creatures which we **had not yet studied might hold** the key to curing certain illnesses.

 Please go to the website for more practice with this structure.

Speaking Activity 15

Work with a partner. Examine what some people have said about the future of mankind. Choose the five statements that you think are most interesting and report these to the class.

"Some men see things as they are and ask why. I dream things that never were and say why not?"

—George Bernard Shaw

"The ultimate test of man's conscience may be his willingness to sacrifice something today for future generations."

—Gaylord Nelson, founder of Earth Day

"I don't think the human race will survive the next thousand years, unless we spread into space."

—Stephen Hawking, cosmologist

"We believe there will be future outposts of humans living elsewhere. I think Mars is a very obvious place for settlement to happen."

—Jeff Greason, CEO and cofounder of XCOR Aerospace

". . . society will be defined not only by what we create but by what we refuse to destroy."

—John Sawhill, former President of The Nature Conservancy

"You must be the change you wish to see in the world."

—Gandhi

"If our long-term survival is at stake, we have a basic responsibility to our species to venture to other worlds."

—Carl Sagan

"One day . . . there will be more humans living off the Earth than on it."

— Michael Griffin, NASA administrator

"We hope to create thousands of astronauts over the next few years and bring alive their dream of seeing the majestic beauty of our planet from above."

—Richard Branson, founder of Virgin Galactic

Speaking Activity 16

Work with a partner. Report on three informal conversations you had recently with classmates, friends, or acquaintances. Get the same information from your partner. You can practise using *say*, *tell*, or *go*.

Conversation With	Direct Speech	Reported Speech
A close friend		
A classmate		
An acquaintance		

SPEAKING STRATEGY

People often start conversations by mentioning something that they heard, something they read about, or something in the news. This is a good strategy to start a conversation.

Speaking Activity 17

Work with a partner. Look at the following news bulletins and practise starting conversations by reporting them. When you have finished, start another conversation by reporting about something you heard or read.

"Population growth, climate change, and demand for greater food and energy supplies are squeezing global water supplies."

—UN report

"A major factor affecting water availability is a surging global population, which may swell to 9 billion by 2050."

—UN report

"Climate change has the potential to change patterns of drought and flooding. In many places, climate-related water events have become more frequent and extreme."

—UN report

"Coping with a future without reliable water resource systems is now a real prospect in parts of the world."

—UN report

"Twenty-five per cent of Africans will face water shortages due to climate change. By 2020, somewhere between 75–250 million people will be suffering from water stress."

—Dr Pauchauri, Intergovernmental Panel on Climate Change

"A total (world) population of 250–300 million people, a 95% decline from present levels, would be ideal."

—Ted Turner, billionaire, founder of CNN

"The only hope for the world is to make sure there is not another United States. We can't let other countries have the same number of cars, the amount of industrialization, we have in the US. We have to stop these Third World countries right where they are."

—Michael Oppenheimer, environmentalist

"I challenge you to see whether there's a legal way of throwing our so-called leaders into jail because what they're doing is a criminal act."

—David Suzuki, scientist

"'Global warming' will kill most of us, and turn the rest of us into cannibals."

—Ted Turner, billionaire, founder of CNN

Communication Focus: Hypothesizing

When we hypothesize, we assume or suppose something will happen if certain conditions exist.

Structure/Expressions	Examples
Future	
If + present tense, . . . will + bare infinitive . . .	*If* there *are* too many people on earth, there *will not be* enough food to feed everyone.
Suppose + present tense, will + bare infinitive . . .	*Suppose* the world population *continues* to grow, *will* there *be* enough food?

Present

If + past tense . . . would + bare infinitive	*If* 10 billion people *inhabited* the planet, there *would be* many environmental problems.
Suppose + past, would + bare infinitve	*Suppose* the earth *became* overcrowded, *would* people *begin* to colonize the moon?
Imagine . . . would + bare infinitve, if + past tense	*Imagine* what *would happen* if the earth's population *reached* 10 billion.

Past

If + past perfect tense, would have + past participle	*If* they *hadn't cut* down the rain forests in that part of Brazil, they *wouldn't have had* enough farm land to grow food.

 Please go to the website for more practice with this structure.

Speaking Activity 18

Work in pairs. Interview your partner. Hypothesize about these situations.

1. If you could live anywhere in the world, where would you live?
2. If you could make one change to the environment, what change would you make?
3. If you could change one thing about yourself, what would you change?
4. If you had been born in North America, how would your life have been different?
5. If you won a lottery which made you rich beyond your wildest dreams, which friends would you stay close to?
6. If you could change places with someone for a month, who would you change places with and why?
7. If cosmetic surgery were available without cost, would you have it? What would you change?
8. If scientists proved that cellphones caused cancer, would you give up your cellphone?
9. If you could have three wishes, what would you ask for?
10. If you had been able to choose any time in history to live in, which period would you have chosen?
11. If you hadn't come to this country, what would you have done?
12. If you had been born the opposite sex, how would your life have been different?
13. What would you do if you have only six months to live?
14. If you could meet and talk to any famous person, living or dead, who would you choose and why?
15. If you could live as long as you wanted to, how long would you like to live and what would you like to accomplish?

Speaking Activity 19

Work in groups. Read the following press releases. There are two possible solutions. One group of experts believes that birth rates must be controlled. The other believes that the earth can provide enough food for all. Decide which group you agree with and state as many hypotheses to support your position as you can.

Examples

For Population Growth: If we established more fish farms and were able to grow vegetables using salt water, we could feed many more people.

For Population Control: Even if we grew food on mountain slopes and in the oceans, we still couldn't provide enough food for another three billion people.

Press Release: Against Population Control

Human rights are part of the very foundation of the modern world. Society, however, seems to have become estranged from its own humanity in that there is a popular idea that there are just too many of us on the planet and that we are responsible for all of its problems. The vocabulary we hear all around us—"the human impact on the environment;" "ecological footprint;" "human consumption"—leaves us feeling guilty, afraid, and apprehensive about the future. Global warming is seen as a direct result of population growth. Does this mean that all the earth's problems would vanish if humans vanished? Many people believe that this focus on limiting population growth takes people's minds away from more productive and creative searches for solutions to hunger, poverty, or the lack of resources. When we ignore or question the truly special qualities of human beings, we are destroying people's confidence in their abilities to tackle the problems of the future. Humans have proved that they can overcome all kinds of problems. Human life is precious and special. How can there possibly be too many humans?

Press Release: For Population Control

As the population has expanded, there are more and more people who consume more resources, and therefore produce more greenhouse gases, more waste, more demands on plants, animals and oceans. All of this results in an increase in global warming. The world population is currently at almost seven billion and could rise to nine billion by 2050 if we continue at the rate we are growing. This will not only threaten the climate, but will cause shortages of food and water, and create armed conflicts. There won't be any progress on the most crucial environmental goals such as reducing carbon emissions, preventing overfishing, and decreasing deforestation unless population growth and its demands on the planet are dealt with. This may bring up other issues that people have different views about such as: abortion, immigration control, economics, and human rights. Nevertheless, it is in the interest of all humanity to stop population growth, if we are to survive as a species.

Your Group's Position	Reasons
_____	_____
_____	_____
_____	_____
_____	_____

Listening 2

Before You Listen

Work with a small group. Discuss the following questions.

1. What is a refugee?

2. What different kinds of refugees have you heard of?

3. Where do the refugees in today's world come from? Why did they leave their countries of origin?

4. How do you think the refugee situation in the world will change in the future?

Pre-listening Vocabulary

You will hear these words and phrases in the interview on the audio CD. Work with a partner or by yourself to write the correct vocabulary next to the definitions.

Vocabulary

energy crisis	to dominate	to switch	migration	intense
drought	decline	doable	to afflict	dispute
to stumble	industrial	reward	desertification	greenhouse gas
hurricane	revolution	runaway	to flee	emissions
affordable	to collapse	immigrants	correspondent	death toll
equator	fossil fuels	irreversible	to fortify	advance guard
	alternative			

Definition	Vocabulary
to strengthen	_____
very strong, extreme	_____
argument, disagreement	_____
release of gases that trap heat in the atmosphere	_____
the number of deaths	_____
not enough energy resources resulting in a serious, unstable crisis situation	_____
troops or soldiers sent ahead of the main army	_____
low cost, can be afforded	_____
a long period of dry weather and lack of rain	_____
to control, govern, rule	_____
severe tropical storm with winds above 75 miles per hour	_____
period of time and socioeconomic change when the main occupations of western countries changed from farming to working in industry and manufacturing	_____
imaginary circle around the circumference of the earth equidistant from both poles	_____

Definition	Vocabulary
organic substances such as oil, gas, coal used for energy or heat	_____
to grow worse	_____
to change	_____
to break down in strength, to fall apart	_____
something given in return for doing a good service	_____
another choice or possibility	_____
people who leave their country of origin for another place	_____
something that has escaped control	_____
act of moving from one region to another	_____
able to be done	_____
transformation of arable land to desert	_____
incapable of being turned back, can not be reversed	_____
person who communicates by writing or reporting	_____
to cause pain or suffering	_____
to almost fall into, to come unexpectedly to,	_____
to escape from	_____

 Listening for the Main Ideas

Background Information

Gwynne Dyer is a Canadian journalist who wrote a book and did a radio series called "Climate Wars," both of which dealt with the geopolitics of climate change. This is what he said about the radio series:

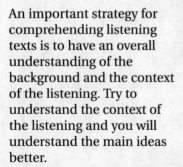

LISTENING STRATEGY

An important strategy for comprehending listening texts is to have an overall understanding of the background and the context of the listening. Try to understand the context of the listening and you will understand the main ideas better.

[A while ago] . . . I noticed that the military in various countries, and especially in the Pentagon, were beginning to take climate change seriously . . . I start[ed] to look into this idea that global warming could lead to wars. It turned into a year-long trek talking to scientists, soldiers, and politicians in a dozen different countries. I have come back . . . seriously worried, and there are . . . things I learned that I think you ought to know.

The first is that a lot of the scientists who study climate change are in a state of suppressed panic these days. Things seem to be moving much faster than their models predicted.

The second thing is that the military strategists are right. Global warming *is* going to cause wars, because some countries will suffer a lot more than others. That will make dealing with the global problem of climate change a lot harder.

The third is that we are probably not going to meet the deadlines. The world's countries will probably not cut their greenhouse gas emissions enough, in time, to keep the warming from going past 2 degrees Celsius. That is very serious . . .

This is NOT a prediction of what the future will look like . . . . It's just a plausible example of what 2046 could look like if we get it wrong over the next ten or fifteen years.

The report you are going to listen to on the audio CD is part of the second report of the series.

 You can find additional information about climate change online.

Listen to the report once and then answer these questions.

1. What crisis does this program describe?

2. What is causing this crisis?

3. In what ways are some countries reacting to the crisis?

4. What is the overall tone of the report? Why do you feel that way?

 Listening Comprehension

Listen to the report again. In the notes below, the main points discussed appear on the left. Some of the details about each point are on the right. As you listen, check the details and add information that is missing. You may want to listen several times. Check your notes with a partner and your teacher.

Main Points	Details
The last energy crisis	prices for charcoal and firewood went up because most of the forests had been cut down
	_____
	_____
	_____
Industrial Revolution in Britain	started when the British substituted coal for wood
	coal was cheaper and better
	_____
	_____
	_____
The current crisis	due to the fact that burning fossil fuels causes climate change
	_____
	_____
	_____
Gwynne Dyer's first experience with climate refugees	three times during 10 days, boats full of refugees sailed onto the tourist beaches in Tenerife, Canary Islands
	_____
	_____
	_____

Main Points	Details
Where the climate refugees come from	40,000 went to the European Union the year before this report
The predicted effects of global warming on the earth	desertification to the south of the US, in Mexico, and in Central America
Michael Clair	professor of Peace and World Security Studies at Hampshire College in Amherst, Massachusetts
The US reaction to climate refugees, according to Michael Clair	when hundreds of millions of refugees travel north, the US will fortify the US– Mexican border
What the destination countries are doing to stop climate refugees	European Union has naval patrols to turn them back and they try to bribe their countries of origin to stop the refugees from leaving
Patty Romero Lancaux	Mexican sociologist working at the national centre for Atmospheric research in Boulder Colorado
Climate predictions	200,000,000 people in Mexico, Central America, and the Caribbean
The pattern Gwynne Dyer sees in the effects of global warming	your most dangerous neighbour is the one who lies between you and the equator
The importance of food	the decline and collapse of almost all great civilizations was due to something that affected the food supply

Main Points	Details
Lester Brown and his opinions about the food supply	grand old man of the environmental movement _____ _____ _____
Why Gwynne Dyer thinks we are lucky	if the crisis had happened 50 years earlier there would have been no major alternatives to fossil fuels available
Gwynne Dyer's conclusions about global warming	we have the technology to stop global warming _____ _____ _____
Dennis Bushnell's conclusions about the crisis	some people think it's too late already _____ _____ _____

Personalizing

Work in small groups of three or four. Here are some quotations from the report. Discuss whether you agree with them or not and explain why. Try to convince the others whose opinions are different from yours.

1. The migration of climate refugees could "change the face of the planet."

2. Imagine . . . the consequences of "what climate change will do to the food supply if warming gets out of control."

3. "Some people think it's too late already [to stop climate change]. Others think we might have 10 years."

Vocabulary and Language Chunks

Write the number of the expression next to the meaning. After checking your answers, choose six expressions and write your own sentences.

Expressions	Meanings
1. go on	☐ to change the appearance of completely
2. run out of	☐ do very well
3. go through the roof	☐ continue
4. do quite well	☐ to finish, use up, have no more left
5. out of control	☐ for us, on our part
6. under control	☐ wait before acting
7. change the face of something	☐ do not try to do
8. come off better	☐ turn out, become
9. weak link	☐ to lose a great deal
10. on our behalf	☐ wait and discover what will happen
11. hold off	☐ the weakest, the least dependable element
12. forget about	☐ able to be controlled
13. take a big hit	☐ cannot be controlled
14. end up	☐ to go beyond, go much higher than expected
15. wait and see	☐ to have a better than expected outcome

🎧 Pronunciation

As we saw in previous chapters, intonation involves the rise and fall of the voice. Intonation patterns are essential for understanding if the speaker has finished speaking or still has more to say. If the speaker has finished, the voice rises and then falls to its lowest pitch level on the last stressed syllable. If the speaker hasn't finished speaking, the voice rises slightly and levels off without falling.

Listen to the speaker on the audio CD read these sentences:

1. Those people are refugees.
2. If a person is a refugee, he or she is protected by many governments.
3. Human rights are important, in modern society.
4. If human rights are important we need to protect them.

In the first and third examples, the speaker's voice falls at the end of the sentences. In the second and fourth sentences, the speaker's voice levels off but the pitch does not fall at the end of the first clause. This shows that the speaker still has more to say and is not finished.

Pronunciation Activity 1

Listen to the sentences on the audio CD and write FINISHED if the voice drops and NOT FINISHED if the voice levels off or rises slightly. Then, write an ending to those sentences which have non final intonation and practise saying all the sentences with a partner.

1. If you are worried about climate change

2. Some people say we still have ten years

3. It's too late already

4. Your most dangerous neighbour

5. Britain became the world's richest country and dominated the world

6. Since these people are moving from poor countries to richer ones

7. As the warming proceeds

8. The destination countries are already taking defensive measures

9. They will follow the well-beaten path and

10. If all the ice melts in the Arctic

11. Due to overfishing there has been a reduction of fish stocks

12. Once the climate warms up three or four degrees

13. In the Arctic, seals are hunted for their fur and meat

14. As soon as North America runs out of water

 Pronunciation Activity 2

Falling intonation signals completeness or certainty, whereas rising intonation signals incompleteness and is used on the first part of complex sentences. Predict the intonation and draw the intonation contours on each part of these sentences. Then listen to the speaker on the audio CD to check your answers, and finally, practise saying these sentences with a partner.

Example

Where there's a will, there's a way.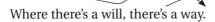

1. You never know until you try.

2. Where there's life, there's hope.

3. When something affected their food supply, civilizations often collapsed.

4. Many refugees drowned while trying to cross the Mediterranean Sea.

5. We started burning fossil fuels two centuries ago and ended up creating a high energy civilization.

6. Global warming is going to cause wars because some countries will suffer a lot more than others.

7. Just because it's doable does not mean that it will be done.

8. If there are severe droughts, people will not be able to make a living from farming.

9. He reports about what climate change will do to the food supply if the warming gets out of control.

10. Canada has resources whereas the USA has money.

11. North Americans are better off than South Americans.

12. As global warming proceeds, winters in Canada will become warmer.

13. Once the industrial revolution took hold, Britain became richer and more powerful.

Pronunciation Activity 3

Intonation can signal choices. Listen to the following sentences on the audio CD. What is the intonation pattern when there is a choice? Please see the Answer Key for the rule.

1. Do you want to see a movie about global warming or about refugees?
2. Will the earth's temperature rise by two degrees or five degrees?
3. Would you rather live in the city or the country?
4. Should we ride bicycles or drive cars?
5. Which do you want to hear first—the bad news or the good news?

Practise repeating these sentences after the speaker on the audio CD. Then work with a partner and write five original sentences which you can ask two other pairs of students. Report your findings to the class.

1. Would you rather be wise or wealthy?
2. Should we go to a concert or to the theatre?
3. Would you like a glass of wine or some beer?
4. Do you want to work in a small company or a large one?
5. Which do you like better, the book or the movie?
6. Did you say it was 10:50 or 10:15?
7. Which would you rather visit, California or Hawaii?
8. Do you feel like walking or driving?
9. Would you rather marry for love or for money?
10. Who do you think is more handsome, Brad Pitt or George Clooney?

Your sentences:

1. _____
2. _____
3. _____
4. _____
5. _____

 Pronunciation Activity 4

There is a specific intonation pattern for lists. Listen to the following sentences on the audio CD and describe the intonation pattern for lists. Please see the Answer Key for the rule.

1. She visited Asia, Africa, South America, and Australia.
2. We want to learn the forms, the meanings, and the uses of the modals.
3. They've bought furniture, appliances, carpets, and plants for their new house.

Work with a partner and predict the intonation pattern on the following sentences. Then listen to the speaker on the audio CD to check your answers. Practise saying the sentences to each other.

1. Helen wants to study Mathematics, Physics, Chemistry, and Biology at university.

2. Andrea bought new scarves, purses, gloves, and jewellery.

3. We need potatoes, carrots, spinach, broccoli, and lettuce.

4. I'd love to visit Argentina, Brazil, Peru, and Uruguay next year.

5. John has never liked soccer, baseball, hockey, or basketball.

Pronunciation Activity 5

This is a game to practise intonation with lists. Work in groups of four or five. Throw a die to determine the subject, according to the following chart. Then throw the die to determine who goes first. The first player must state two items from the category. For example, if the number thrown is 4, the category is fruit, so the first player will name two fruits. The next player will repeat the first two items and add the name of another fruit, and so on. When the students cannot think of any other words, they can choose a new category. The group scores a point for each word in the category and the group with the highest total points wins.

Number	Category	Points
1	Cities you want to visit	_____
2	Countries you want to see	_____
3	Vegetables	_____
4	Fruit	_____
5	Stores or businesses	_____
6	What to do to be a successful student	_____

Other possible categories: sports, actors, colours, animals, languages, and how to make friends.

 ## Pronunciation Activity 6

Listen to the dialogues. Why were there two different answers? Please check the Answer Key for the answer.

A: I'm renting a place in Toronto.
B: Where?
A: In Scarborough.

A: I'm renting a place in Toronto.
B: Where?
A: In Toronto.

A: I'm going out to eat.
B: Where?
A: McDonald's.

A: I'm going out to eat.
B: Where?
A: Out to eat.

Work with a partner. In this activity, student A answers with a question word with either rising or falling intonation. Student B then answers giving either more specific information or just repeating the statement. Take turns and practise both kinds of intonation, and the correct responses to each. The first four have been done for you to use as examples.

1. I'll do this as soon as I finish my work.

   Question word   **Response**

   When?   At six o'clock.

   Question word   **Response**

   When?   As soon as I finish my work.

2. The World Wildlife Fund supports research in the Canadian wilderness.

   Question word   **Response**

   Where?   In the Canadian wilderness.

   Question word   **Response**

   Where?   In Nunavut.

3. Animal rights organizations are fighting to protect Canada's endangered species in the north.

   Question word   **Response**

   What?   Polar bears.

   Question word   **Response**

   What?   Animal rights organizations are fighting to protect Canada's endangered. species.

4. Scientists claim that global warming will cause crops to decrease in the future.

   Question word   **Response**

   What?   Grains and vegetables.

   Question word   **Response**

   What?   Global warming will cause crops to decrease.

5. There was a terrible earthquake in Chile.

   Question word   **Response**

   _____   _____

   Question word   **Response**

   _____   _____

6. I forgot my back pack at school.

   Question word   **Response**

   _____   _____

   Question word   **Response**

   _____   _____

7. I'll see you next Thursday.

   Question word   **Response**

   _____   _____

   Question word   **Response**

   _____   _____

8. Let's have dinner on the weekend.

   Question word   **Response**

   _____   _____

   Question word   **Response**

   _____   _____

9. I'm going to the sports complex.

   Question word   **Response**

   _____   _____

   Question word   **Response**

   _____   _____

10. I want to buy a gift for my teacher.

    Question word   **Response**

    _____   _____

    Question word   **Response**

    _____   _____

Pronunciation: Thought Groups

In a sentence, words can be divided into shorter meaningful units which can be called thought groups. Listen to these examples on the audio CD and try to determine how we signal thought groups. Please see the Answer Key for the rule.

1. It's not difficult to conserve resources and protect the environment.
2. Man is responsible for polluting the earth and destroying species.
3. How much more destruction can nature and the environment bear?
4. There are many things we can do to preserve the balance of nature and the environment.

Pronunciation Activity 7

Work with a partner. Tell each other about three things you do to protect the environment. Mention how often and why you do them. Then join another pair of students and find out about their efforts to protect the environment. Report the most interesting or unusual actions to the class. Try to use thought group intonation.

What I Do	How Often I Do It	Why I Do It

Communicating in the Real World

Try to use your English to talk to people outside your class. Work with a partner to make up a questionnaire asking four to eight questions about one of the following topics. Show your questions to the teacher. Then speak to people who are not in your class and report to the class what you learned.

Topics: pets and animals, WWF and PETA, endangered species, cars and pollution, global warming and climate change, overpopulation, and refugees.

Self Evaluation

Rate yourself and write your comments in each of the sections of the chart. Show the chart to your teacher.

Topic	Good (5, 4)	Improving (3, 2)	Needs more work (1, 0)
Grammar and Language Functions 1. Taking turns in conversation 2. Using the passive voice 3. Expressing disapproval 4. Criticizing 5. Eliciting and analyzing opinions expressing various degrees of certainty 6. Persuading and countering arguments 7. Expressing regrets 8. Reporting information 9. Hypothesizing and conditionals			
Speaking Strategies 1. When you are speaking, take a chance and try to express your ideas if you have something you want to say. Don't worry about sounding foolish or making mistakes. The most important thing is to get your idea across.			

Topic	Good (5, 4)	Improving (3, 2)	Needs more work (1, 0)
2. People often start conversations by mentioning something that they heard or read about, or something in the news. This is a good strategy for you to get a conversation going. 3. What other speaking strategies did you use?			
Listening Strategies 1. Listen for the feelings and emotions behind the message. Understanding the emotions of the speakers can help you figure out the main ideas. 2. An important strategy for comprehending listening texts is to have an overall understanding of the background and the context of the listening. Try to understand the context of the listening and you will understand the main ideas better. 3. What other listening strategies did you use?			
Pronunciation More on intonation			

Vocabulary and Language Chunks

Write 10 sentences using vocabulary from the chapter.

1. _____
2. _____
3. _____
4. _____
5. _____
6. _____
7. _____
8. _____
9. _____
10. _____

My plan for practising is . . . _____

_____

_____

Answer Key

Chapter 1

Speaking Activity 13, page 11

Yellow: You are happy, positive, optimistic, relaxed, and carefree. You are social and hard-working. You find life easy.

Red: You have strong feelings and are energetic. You are impulsive and have a lot of ambition. You are a good leader. You want to live life fully.

Green: You are helpful and scientific. You don't like change. You are persistent and sometimes jealous and selfish. You worry about failure.

Brown: You are honest, practical, and supportive. Security is important to you. You are restless. You think a lot about your health.

Blue: You are calm, peaceful, loyal, sensitive, and easily hurt. You are in control of your life. You are content. You want a simple and worry-free life.

Black: You are serious. You like to make your own decisions and don't like to be told what to do.

Grey: You are uncommitted and neutral. You are an observer, not a doer. You are cautious and passive.

Violet: You often have conflicts. You are interested in the mystical. You are spiritual and understanding.

Orange: You are competent, very neat, organized, and fair.

White: You are individualistic, lonely, and have strong opinions. You sometimes have difficulty making friends.

Pink: You are sensitive and easily hurt. You try to do your best. Sometimes you are a little immature. You want people to like you.

Speaking Activity 19, page 18

If you answered TRUE to 1, 3, 6, 7, 8, 16, 17, you are motivated and you work hard at improving your English.

14 and 15 are probably true for most people.

If you answered TRUE to 2, 4, 5, 9, 10, 11, 12, 13, try to take more responsibility for your learning. Find things that you like about learning and speaking English. Motivate yourself and try to develop your English personality. Don't worry about grammar so much.

Pronunciation Activity 1, page 19

opti**mis**tic
intro**duc**tion
ener**get**ic
characte**ris**tic
communi**ca**tion
se**cu**rity
enthusi**as**tic
de**li**cious
occu**pa**tion
conver**sa**tion
de**ci**sion
o**pi**nion
indi**vi**dual
com**mer**cial
syste**ma**tic
ro**ma**ntic
ex**pre**ssion
con**clu**sion
at**ten**tion
curious
oppor**tu**nity
individua**lis**tic

famili**ar**ity

ne**ce**ssity

passion

compre**hen**sion

gram**ma**tical

cou**ra**geous

super**sti**tious

am**bi**tious

a**bil**ity

origin**al**ity

practical

comical

psycho**log**ical

gorgeous

Rule: When words end with one of the suffixes *–ic, –ical, –ity, –tion, –ial, –sial, –cial, –ious, –cious,* or *–eous,* the stress is put on the syllable which comes directly before the suffix.

Pronunciation Activity 2, page 19

table

button

handle

lettuce

illness

cousin

pumpkin

garden

picture

barrel

zipper

turkey

apron

pocket

blanket

pillow

jacket

ceiling

scissors

folder

carpet

purpose

kitchen

Rule: In English nouns of two syllables, the stress falls on the first syllable in more than 90 per cent of all cases.

Pronunciation Activity 3, page 20

airport

driveway

greenhouse

blackboard

haircut

armchair

ashtray

bookstore

classroom

headache

toenail

raincoat

bluebird

doorbell

bookcase

backpack

sunglasses

blackbird

eyebrow

Rule: These are compound nouns. In compound nouns, the major stress falls on the stressed syllable of the first noun.

Pronunciation Activity 4, page 20

es**cape**

ad**mire**

su**ggest**

sur**vive**

o**ffend**

for**give**

for**get**

re**quest**

im**prove**

sur**prise**

re**place**

a**rrest**

at**tract**

re**ceive**

con**clude**

res**pect**

pro**tect**

re**peat**

con**tain**

de**cide**

im**prove**

ad**mit**

a**nnounce**

Rule: In verbs containing two syllables, the stress falls on the second syllable in about 60 per cent of the cases.

Pronunciation Activity 5, page 20

Rule: If the word is a noun, the stress falls on the first syllable. If the word is a verb, the stress falls on the second syllable.

Chapter 2

Pronunciation Activity 2, page 44

1. needed   /Id/
   wanted   /Id/
   started   /Id/
   ended   /Id/
   invited   /Id/
   added   /Id/
   visited   /Id/
   decided   /Id/

Rule: When the verb ends with a /t/ or /d/, the past tense is pronounced /Id/.

2. washed   /t/
   laughed   /t/
   fished   /t/
   liked   /t/
   talked   /t/
   bumped   /t/
   watched   /t/
   finished   /t/
   stuffed   /t/
   stopped   /t/
   helped   /t/
   coughed   /t/
   danced   /t/
   ranked   /t/
   hiked   /t/
   tripped   /t/
   punched   /t/
   dressed   /t/

Rule: When the verb ends with a voiceless consonant, pronounce the past tense ending as /t/.

3. lived   /d/
   closed   /d/
   wandered   /d/
   tried   /d/
   rained   /d/
   roamed   /d/
   called   /d/
   played   /d/
   viewed   /d/
   showed   /d/
   smiled   /d/
   answered   /d/
   cried   /d/
   starred   /d/
   cycled   /d/

Rule: When the verb ends with a voiced sound, pronounce the past tense ending as /d/.

Chapter 3

Listening 2 Pre-listening Activity, page 65

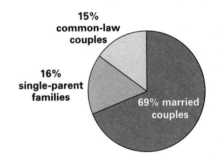

15% common-law couples

16% single-parent families

69% married couples

Chapter 4

Pronunciation Activity 2, page 97

There was a <u>young</u> <u>lady</u> whose <u>chin</u>,
<u>Resembled</u> the <u>point</u> of a <u>pin</u>.
So she <u>had</u> it <u>made</u> <u>sharp</u>,
And <u>purchased</u> a <u>harp</u>,
And <u>played</u> <u>many</u> <u>tunes</u> with her <u>chin</u>.

There was an <u>old</u> <u>man</u> with a <u>beard</u>,
Who <u>said</u>, "It is <u>just</u> as I <u>feared!</u>—
Two <u>owls</u> and a <u>hen</u>,
Four <u>larks</u> and a <u>wren</u>,
Have all <u>built</u> their <u>nests</u> in my <u>beard!</u>"

Chapter 6

Speaking Activity 18, page 141

1. c
2. b
3. a
4. c
5. c
6. a
7. b
8. a

Chapter 7

Thinking and Talking, page 156

1. (a) is the correct answer. The OK gesture is considered very rude in Brazil. However, in North America and England it means everything is just great.

2. (c) is the correct answer. When a French person does this, the meaning is, "I don't believe you." Think of it as being similar to an English speaker who doesn't believe something and says, "My eye!"

3. (a) is the correct answer. This gesture is fine to use to beckon to someone in North America. However, it is very rude in Asian countries.

4. The correct answer is (c). This stance can also mean extreme arrogance in many Asian countries.

5. (b) is the correct answer. Although this gesture means everything is OK in North America and Europe, it is an extremely rude gesture in Iran and other Middle Eastern countries.

6. (c) is the correct answer. People from Egypt and other Middle Eastern countries consider the foot the lowest and therefore the most unclean part of the body, so it is very rude to show the sole of the foot. This is also true in Thailand.

7. (a) is the correct answer. This is a gesture for "no" in many Middle Eastern countries.

8. (c) is the correct answer. This is not usual behaviour in the other countries mentioned.

9. (a) is the correct answer. Although this gesture means "stop" in North America and Europe, in Asia it is a gesture used when requesting permission to speak.

10. (c) is the correct answer. Picking your nose is not considered rude in China, particularly when done by older people. Younger people are more westernized and probably wouldn't do this.

Pronunciation Activity 7, page 181

Chart B

	Canada	USA
Head of government		
Total area	9,984,670 square kilometres	9,826,530 square kilometres
Size of population		
GDP (gross domestic product) per capita		
Disposable income per capita	$28,591 US	$34,949 US
Life expectancy	81.2 years	78.1 years
Nobel Prize winners	10	270

Chapter 8

Speaking Activity 3, page 186

All the statements are true.

Speaking Activity 10, page 197

1. True. Women have a larger deep limbic system than men, which allows them to be more in touch with their feelings and better able to express them. They can feel greater happiness and also greater sadness and depression.

2. True. Females develop language skills earlier than males and they keep this edge all their lives. Two sections of the brain responsible for language are larger in women than in men, indicating one reason that women excel in language. Additionally, men typically only process language in their dominant hemisphere, whereas women process language in both hemispheres.

3. True. While women have better coordination doing precise delicate tasks, men are more accurate when taking aim at a target.

4. True. Women communicate more effectively than men, focusing on how to create a solution that everyone agrees with, using non-verbal cues such as tone, emotion, and empathy; men tend to be more task-oriented, less talkative, and more isolated.

5. True. Men have stronger spatial abilities, and are able to mentally represent a shape and its dynamics, whereas women usually struggle in this area. Men have a stronger ability to read a map without turning it around. Women find their way by paying attention to landmarks.

6. True. An area of the brain called the inferior-parietal lobule (IPL) is larger in men than in women, especially on the left side. This section of the brain is thought to control mental mathematical ability, and probably explains why men frequently perform better in mathematical tasks than women.

7. True. Men are generally stronger with left-brain activities and approach problem-solving from a task-oriented perspective while women typically solve problems more creatively and are more aware of feelings while communicating.

8. True. Women can recall a dream in more detail. Men's dreams take place outdoors and in unfamiliar places. Women's dreams often take place in familiar places and indoors. Men see twice as many males in their dreams as females, but women see an equal number of both sexes. Men tend to have more strangers, identified by their occupations in their dreams, whereas women dream about people they know socially, such as family members, coworkers, or friends.

9. True. According to a study in Britain, men tell twice as many lies as women. Researchers found that, on average, a man tells six lies a day to his partner, boss, and work colleagues, but a woman tells just three on average.

10. True. Men have a "fight or flight" response to stress situations while women seem to approach these situations with a "tend and befriend" strategy. During times of stress women take care of themselves and their children (tending) and form strong group bonds (befriending).

Language Studies International
1055 Yonge St., Suite 210
Toronto, ON M4W 2L2
Tel: 416-928-6888 Fax: 416-928-3388
Email: tor@lsi.edu Web: www.lsi.edu